What people are saying about this book:

This book offers a simple, accessible, and truly profound opportunity for people to see how to recognize and fulfill the potential in what could always be an energizing relationship, a true meeting of the minds expressed through meaningful, productive meetings. I recommend it to everyone who spends time with others to achieve a common objective. —**Judith A. Sedgeman**, Director, The Sydney Banks Institute for Innate Health at the Robert C. Byrd Health Sciences Center, West Virginia University

The missing link of meetings–what's really important. —**Bob Grace**, Group Leader, ESA, Los Alamos National Laboratories

The meeting techniques combined with a greater understanding of listening as described in this book can definitely improve the performance of any organization. —**Tom Nielsen**, CEO, Kennewick General Hospital

Managers should add this book to their understanding of what makes for effective meetings. —**Walter Scott**, Retired CEO

Want to fix meetings—the process with the most waste, redundancy, and inconsistency? Read this book and see how you can use the principles that will not only transform the quality of your meetings but also will enable you to work with anyone gracefully and easily—no matter how difficult they seem to you now! —**Robert Gunn**, Founder, Gunn Partners (Exult company)

DEDICATED TO...

...every leader, manager, supervisor and employee who spends too much time in too many meetings with too few results.

We've Got To Start Meeting Like This!

How To Get Better Results With Fewer Meetings

Robert C. Kausen

First Edition

Life Education®, Inc. • Coffee Creek, CA

LEi

We've Got To Start Meeting Like This!

How To Get Better Results With Fewer Meetings

Robert C. Kausen

Published by:
Life Education, Inc.
HCR 2 Box 3969
Trinity Center, CA 96091-9500 U.S.A.

Orders 530/266-3235 or orders@life-education.com

© 2003

ISBN 0-945787-50-2

First Printing 2003

Printed in the United States of America

Library of Congress Cataloging-in-Publication Data

Kausen, Robert C.

We've go to start meeting like this! : how to get better results with fewer meetings / Robert C. Kausen. -- 1st ed.

p. cm.
Includes index.
LCCN 2002092910
ISBN 0-945787-50-2

1. Business meetings. 2. Interpersonal Relations.
3. Leadership—Psychological aspects. I. Title.

HF5734.5.K38 2002   658.4'56
                        QBI02-200562

CONTENTS

Foreword by Kevin Gleason   7
President and CEO, Adams Outdoor Advertising
Meet Robert Kausen   9
Acknowledgment   11

WARM UP

IS THIS BOOK FOR YOU?   14

1 ANOTHER MEETING BOOK?   17
Not Exactly!

A FOUNDATION FOR UNDERSTANDING

2 REFLECTIVE LISTENING   23
Getting to the Heart of Matters

3 HIGH-PERFORMANCE STATES   35
From Grace to the Zone

4 WHAT GOES ON BETWEEN THE EARS   40
A Peek Under the Hood

5 WE ARE FISH IN WATER   55
Invisible Influences

6 INNATE HEALTH, COMMON SENSE,   65
AND CREATIVITY
It's all Natural

7 TRACKING THE SIGNS OF   70
HIGH-PERFORMANCE THINKING
Built-in Compass

8 WHAT MAKES A GOOD MEETING?   77
Tangible Intangibles

DYNAMICS

9 PERSON TO PERSON   83
Relationship Essentials

10 CONFLICT EVOLUTION   94
A Meeting of the Minds

11 DECISION-INDECISION   103
Teeter-Totter of Turmoil

12 OPINIONS   109
Meeting Catapult or Quagmire

13 BRAINSTORMING   116
Tapping Original Thought

THE MECHANICS

14 TO MEET OR NOT TO MEET   124
A Classic Question Worth Remembering

15 WHO SHOULD ATTEND   132
Time to Get Off Automatic

16 GIVING NOTICE   137
Starting Off on the Right Foot

17 DOCUMENTING THE MEETING   145
Brief and to the Point

IN CONCLUSION

18 GUIDING THE MEETING TONE   153
Sensing When and How to Intervene

19 YOU'RE IT   162
What if No One Else Understands this Stuff?

20 PUTTING IT ALL TOGETHER   172
It's Just Common Sense

RESOURCES

Suggested Meeting Rules   178
Resources for Further Learning   179
Index   185

FOREWORD

Remember when you were a child?

Think of the meetings you used to go to... Little League, scouts, student government. Do you remember what those experiences felt like? Were they positive, comfortable, and enjoyable?

Since early childhood, I can remember going to one kind of meeting or another, most of which seemed to be a natural part of my youth. I enjoyed the meeting experience back then, because part of the time was devoted to discussing the "important stuff" with friends, classmates, teammates—and even family.

The key ingredients of these meetings seemed to be good camaraderie, interesting content, and the magic that is created when people get together and bring new ideas and insights into the world. No one seemed too judgmental, overly serious, or heavy-handed! The focus was on the common good and not on an agenda.

Fast forward to my first real job—a major advertising agency outside Detroit. Creative meetings, account meetings, budget meetings, scheduling meetings, performance reviews, meetings to determine what was said at the last meeting...and on and on and on. It's exhausting just thinking about it.

And although I've traveled through various businesses and companies since my days in the ad biz, the meeting dynamic didn't change for me until I came upon what I consider to be a life-changing understanding. This understanding is the foundation for Robert Kausen's book, *We've Got to Start Meeting Like This!*

This is an understanding that holds dear the human factor and the individual's ability to think and create original thought. It is an understanding that cherishes wisdom over intellect and creativity over content. It is an understanding that sees the world as a universe of possibilities and not a set of limitations.

It is an understanding that has changed me and changed the company I work for in a powerful way.

This book will take the reader on a journey of discovery, illuminating the benefits of a healthy state of mind in today's business world. The concepts in this book will transcend the memory-based intelligence of the reader and promote a deeper level of thought where creativity and inspiration originate.

As President of the fourth largest outdoor advertising company in the United States, I feel unbelievably fortunate to have been introduced to this principle-based understanding back in the early '90s. It has changed the culture of our organization dramatically—creating an environment where people are happier and more productive than ever without the fear factor that permeates the climate of most businesses. The "meeting" experience is the conduit for this understanding.

Imagine walking out of your next meeting feeling absolutely inspired, regardless of the content or objectives. Imagine being able to tackle the most difficult business issues in a meeting environment where everyone feels connected and enthusiastic. Imagine being able to achieve higher performance and greater levels of productivity in less time with less friction and stress.

This book is not a tactical approach to more successful meetings, even though it outlines certain mechanics that can elevate your next meeting. In a bigger picture, this book focuses on one's ability to THINK and the awesome power behind thought. What if you could evoke everyone's best thinking at your next meeting? Good idea? If so, I highly recommend opening your mind to the possibilities awaiting you in this book. I think you'll find yourself reading it many times.

—Kevin Gleason,
President and CEO, Adams Outdoor Advertising

MEET ROBERT KAUSEN

My professional career started in the world of chemistry—and that probably started with my first chemistry set at the age of nine or ten. A few loud explosions and mother's copper plated oven

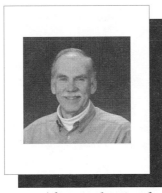

almost ended that career. After graduating from Cal Tech in 1956 with a major in applied chemistry and a minor in girls, I served for four years in the US Army Counter Intelligence Corps as an intelligence specialist and German linguist. In 1960, I landed a job with the world-renowned Arthur D. Little, Inc. in Cambridge, Massachusetts—an incredible group of creative R&D folks specializing in everything from basic research to state-of-the-art product development.

In 1964, I moved back to California and went to work as a structural adhesive formulator for Narmco Materials (now a division of CIBA Geigy), manufacturers of structural adhesives and reinforced plastics. Over the next 12 years, I gained a lot of experience working with people in my capacity as manager of several departments including Process Engineering, Adhesives Manufacturing, Graphite Tape Manufacture, and Quality Assurance.

Along the way, I became increasingly curious about how to most effectively work with people. As evidenced by union grievances, much of what I was doing clearly did not work well, and the sparse management training offered in those years by the company helped very little. So I started exploring resources and trainings in

Southern California. Along the way, I came to increasingly respect the power and potential of the human mind.

By 1976, I was already spending some of my weekends each month learning to become a personal development trainer with a small Southern California firm. To my amazement, I became so enthralled with helping people realize more of their potential that I left my technical career in 1977. As the company grew, I eventually became Director of Training. In 1981, I left the firm became VP and Director of Training for an international consulting and business training firm.

In 1980, I had a chance to hear author Sydney Banks speak—an event that changed my entire view of helping people. All my training and work had been problem-focused—based on the notion that life happened to us and we had to deal with it. For example, stress came from people and circumstances. During that life-changing weekend, I came to realize that it was exactly the opposite. *Life experience is created from the inside out. I needed to focus on people's innate mental health!*

In 1982, I established Life Education®, Inc. as a vehicle to bring this profound understanding to individuals and organizations . Our purpose is to assist leaders to align people behind the organization's vision and mission and to bring out the best in people. All of our programs are based on the principles discussed in this book. We create programs specific to issues an organization faces (such as communications, customer service, sales, quality, and teamwork, dealing with difficult personalities). Our programs are geared toward changing the entire human relations climate. The Life Education®, Inc. Website, http://www.life-education.com contains extensive information on our programs. My Last book was *Customer Satisfaction Guaranteed.*

My wife, DeeDee, and I have been together since 1970. Each of us brought three wonderful children into our marriage (for a total of six in the newly formed family), and we now enjoy 12 grandchildren—and counting. At every opportunity, I love to fly-fish in our many streams and coax bass from nearby Trinity Lake.

MY DEEP GRATITUDE GOES TO...

First and foremost, Sydney Banks—author, theosopher, mentor, and dear friend—who has generously spent time and energy over the past 22 years helping me achieve an ever-deepening understanding of the principles that are the foundation of this book.

Kevin Gleason, President and CEO of Adams Outdoor Advertising, for his valuable input and the sterling Foreword that attests to the practicality of this understanding.

Judith Sedgeman for her helpful review of the integrity and clarity of the principles presented in this book.

The following clients and colleagues who have taken the time to read drafts and offer essential feedback and suggestions: Dick Bozoin, Jim Cherveny, Reese Coppage, Frank Gallinaro, Bob Grace, Bob Gunn, John Hirsch, Charlie Kiefer, Karen McGinnis, Paul Nakai, Tom Nielsen, Joe SanFilippo, Ralf Schirg, Walter Scott, and Brian Taylor.

Richard Carlson, best-selling author of *Don't Sweat the Small Stuff* and many others, for his review and kind endorsement that appears on the cover.

Bill Marvin for the delightful title idea and his infectious sense of humor.

My colleague, friend, and former partner, George Pransky, for putting me on the trail of this understanding back in the 1970's and for his friendship and mentoring over the years. His insights about decisions were especially influential in Chapter 11. Linda Pransky has been a valued teacher and inspiration over the years.

The thousands of clients who continue to entrust me with their employees, providing an amazing opportunity to continue to deepen my own understanding.

Laurie Viera whose editorial skills played a major role in keeping this book simple and readable without diluting the power of this understanding. Robin Quinn and her staff were most helpful in making sure the punctuation made sense.

Especially to my wife of 30 years, DeeDee, who often wondered how I could possibly be working *and* enjoying just sitting in front of a computer. I wasn't working, just playing.

WARM UP

IS THIS BOOK FOR YOU?

A better question might be *"Do you want to learn how to hold fewer meetings, shorter meetings, and get better results?"*

Ever since primitive man gathered to arrange hunts and talk about matters of tribal importance, people have been meeting. When people meet, they hope to experience understanding, fellowship, creativity, and synergy that are not possible alone. However, in recent decades, the world of business has added new meanings to the meeting process. "Meeting" may now also conjure images of dread, boredom, and confrontation.

Still, today's business world has gone meeting mad. When I first begin working with a company, it is not uncommon for me to find mid- to high-level managers spending over 70% of their time in meetings. And for the most part, most of them feel that over half the meetings are a total waste of time. To put this meeting madness into career perspective, 70% of a manager's time means about three days a week, or 50,000 hours in a typical career, spent most often with only marginal results. Even if we optimistically say that 50% of meeting time is effective, this means that 25,000 hours of a manager's time are wasted during a typical career. For a $50,000 manager, this would mean over a half million dollars wasted in a career. And that is for just one mid-level manager.

Because so little is accomplished in most meetings, managers are working longer hours to handle their expanding workload. It's little wonder that there are increasing feelings of frustration and powerlessness in so many managers.

You might ask why we don't abolish meetings altogether. You'll see that I actually suggest that, in some instances. However, running (or eliminating) business meetings is not my profession. My work is teaching people how to use their thinking in a more effective manner. I show executives, managers, and supervisors how to reach high-performance states of mind and how to bring out the best in themselves and others. I do this by teaching them how to access their innate, creative, and responsive power of healthy, creative thought. Because the people I work with spend so much of their time in meetings, this environment is the most logical place to start using the principles I teach them.

This book casts meetings in a new light and brings a refreshingly commonsense understanding to the issue. You may also recognize that these principles apply in most every aspect of your life.

As I observe business meetings, I notice that most managers do not understand the basics of relationships, human functioning, and group dynamics—in other words, they do not understand the role of thinking in performance and results. At some point in my corporate consulting work and executive development coaching, I usually teach clients about the critical nature of the human factor in successful meetings. For example, in talking with one of my clients, the Chief Operating Officer of a large health care organization, I learned that people left some of his meetings with feelings of resentment. This disclosure puzzled me, because he is a very savvy, humane, yet firm manager. Upon exploration, we discovered that he did not know how to present decisions to a group in a way that would not generate bad feelings later on. When I explained to him what you will learn in Chapter 11 about decisions, this executive immediately realized where he got in trouble. This man changed the way he handled decisions in meetings, and he solved the problem.

Understanding the basic principles governing the human factor (how thought works and why people think and behave as they do) makes it possible for managers to run short, effective, and less frequent meetings. I know this book will be of great interest and value to anyone involved with meetings. It is a fresh look beyond mechanics and techniques. With the understanding you will gain from this book, mechanics and techniques take on a deeper meaning.

Even though what I am pointing to here is just common sense (the obvious in light of a wiser perspective), as you grasp the understanding in this book you will see ways to better leverage your meetings into highly productive *and* enjoyable times. So turn the page and enjoy the journey.

I welcome your feedback and suggestions and will consider them for future editions.

Robert C. Kausen
Coffee Creek, California

1

ANOTHER MEETING BOOK?
Not Exactly!

This is not another book of techniques for running meetings. This book is about understanding how to bring out the best thinking in people—how to assist them to operate in highly effective states of mind. Using the principle-based understanding in this book leads to fewer meetings and ones that are shorter and more effective.

For purposes of this book, I am defining a meeting as a scheduled gathering of more than two people. Technically, when two people come together it is a meeting—and everything in this book about the human factor certainly applies. However, in this book I will focus on meetings involving three or more people.

A successful meeting is one in which the spirit is upbeat, the purpose is fulfilled, and people feel good about the time they have spent. In my corporate consulting work and executive development coaching, however, I often find that people feel worse after meetings than they did before. This is a certain sign that the flames of insecure thinking have been fanned in those meeting. In fact, it now seems clear that done poorly, meetings are the delivery system for insecurity, fears, and doubts in organizations.

Yet done well, they can be the delivery system for inspiration, health, and well-being. If this is not obvious to you now, I think it will be before you finish this book.

Here is a puzzling fact. A recent search of Amazon.com returned over 1,100 matches for the topic of "meetings" and over 350 matches for "business meetings." Of the first 50 matches, at least 40 purport to tell the reader how to run better meetings. If there is so much written about meetings—no doubt filled with good advice based on experience—then why haven't those good ideas and techniques resulted in a major, universal improvement in meeting productivity and quality? What stands in the way? You will discover, as I have, that what stands in the way is a lack of UNDERSTANDING. Techniques and information without a foundation of understanding are about as useful as a skeleton without flesh, blood, nerves, and a brain.

From my work with organizations and individual executives over the past 20 years, I believe that the key to successful meetings lies in how well people understand the human factor; that is, the wise use of thinking and its resulting state of mind.

The reason so many well-intentioned books and programs effect little change is that information and techniques rarely change thinking. Modifying behavior is a tough route.

But when a person's thinking changes, then everything changes. Changing thought requires insight. Insight results in a shift of perspective. Only when thinking evolves can attitude, behavior, performance, and results change permanently. So if you are looking for a book full of techniques and platitudes, this isn't it. But if you would like to gain a wiser understanding of how to become a more potent thinker—an understanding that has proven to boost individual and organizational effectiveness—then I invite you to read on and find your own good ideas. Once you have some understanding of the basic principles governing the human factor (the creative power of original thought and its connection to state of mind and results), you will be able to run shorter, more productive, and more uplifting meetings. While mechanics and techniques are not the major focus of this book, I will talk about a few in the light of a deeper understanding.

What I am offering in this book is what might be called common sense, practical wisdom, or even enlightened intelligence. Of course, common sense is not really all that common. Sometimes I write something and think, "That is so obvious that it will insult my readers." Yet I've learned over the years that the "obvious" is often the most helpful—and the most profound.

This is not just another book about meetings. This is a book about understanding people at a deeper level and putting that understanding to effective use in meetings.

Getting the most from this book

When my colleagues and I teach teams of business people how to use your thinking more effectively, the result is shorter meetings with more punch and greater enjoyment. Once you understand the critical factors and principles, everything else becomes obvious. To help you get a handle on the basic understanding, I often make the same point in several different ways. I'm not just repeating myself—it often takes several ways of talking about the basics before people click into the understanding. That is the nature of learning by insight and realization. But once you catch on, you will recognize that it is not difficult, it is *elegantly simple!*

The logic and layout

I have laid out the book in what I think is a logical sequence from a learning point of view.

The **WARMUP** section contains this segment and Chapter 1. They tell you what this book is and is not about.

A FOUNDATION FOR UNDERSTANDING section lays out the foundation and principles of this approach in Chapters 2-8.

The **DYNAMICS** section covers the principles and dynamics of human interactions in Chapters 9-13.

The **MECHANICS** section covers the practical application of the understanding and dynamics in Chapters 14-18.

The **IN CONCLUSION** section pulls everything together in Chapters 18-20, and an Appendix follows providing Resources.

To get the most from this book, I urge you to get a good grasp of the FOUNDATION FOR UNDERSTANDING and DYNAMICS sections before you go further. After that, everything else is laid out in a logical order starting with whether to even hold a meeting. If a particular item interests you, feel free to jump around once you have read the first two sections.

So, relax, get the gist of things and let the understanding come to you. It *is* that simple.

Summing up

This book focuses on understanding how to use your thinking more effectively so you can draw people toward highly effective states of mind. That is the route to more effective, shorter, and fewer meetings. The way to get the most from this book is to get a good grasp of the understanding and principles that form its foundation. The practical applications handled in later chapters will take on a new, wiser meaning in light of that deeper understanding of the human factor.

A great many people think they are thinking when they are merely rearranging their prejudice.

— **William James**

Coming up...

In the next chapter, we will jump right into an in-depth look at listening. If the only thing you gain from this book is to become an even more effective listener, then you will improve every relationship in your life and every meeting you attend.

A FOUNDATION FOR
UNDERSTANDING

2

REFLECTIVE LISTENING
Getting to the Heart of Matters

If people don't feel understood, they are seldom open to input. You cannot truly hear and understand when you are actively thinking about anything—including your response, judgments, implications, and applications of what you are hearing. This clear state of mind is valuable in reading a book like this as well!

We will start out with a look at listening because it is a key skill required to run successful meetings, and to foster successful relationships of all kinds. The same principles of a clear and present state of mind will help you get the most out of this book as well. Let's start with a look at the most common types of listening that we experience day-to-day.

Listening without hearing

How many times have you attended a meeting that was locked in hot disagreement, only to realize that the protagonists are pretty much in agreement but can't hear it? This scenario is a common one because people seldom truly listen to one another. People love to talk about their own ideas and views, but most people don't know how to listen well to others. Almost anyone can follow the content of a conversation, but it takes a deeper understanding to get the full meaning.

Consider your own experience. How often in a meeting, or even in a personal conversation, do you feel truly *understood*? How often do you walk away saying, "He didn't really listen to me. He didn't get it." If you think you are a great listener, check it out by asking your mate!

Listening to evaluate

This content-oriented, critical form of listening is so common that it probably seems normal to most people. Inside your head it looks something like this: As the other person says something, you quickly and efficiently evaluate/judge what he is saying. The moment-to-moment result of this process is that you either agree or disagree with what the other person is saying. If you agree, you will likely turn your thinking toward examples of your own that support what he has said. If you disagree, you will likely turn your thinking toward how to rebut his statements. This process limits your ability to go deeper and gain a truer understanding of what the other person is trying to communicate. In effect, you stop listening.

Now let's look at some deeper notions about listening. You will see that deeper listening—what I refer to as insightful or reflective listening—is a critical part of influencing any meeting in a more productive direction.

Getting to the heart of matters

As a listener, reflective listening provides the opportunity for you to expand your own view and understanding. After you understand what the speaker has said (and the speaker agrees that you do), then you can accept or reject, debate, or expand. Reflective listening is sometimes challenging because of all of the thinking habits we have accumulated. To listen so that the *speaker feels understood,* you cannot allow yourself any extraneous thinking. For example, you cannot indulge in evaluation, judgment, implications, applications, or memories. It is essential that you be fully present with the other person, absorbing what she has to say without agreeing or disagreeing. You pose questions only to better understand and fully grasp the position of the speaker.

Listening to clarify

How we feel about issues and what we think about them are usually not well-defined in our heads until we start to speak. Indeed, we may hold two contradictory ideas simultaneously without realizing it. Similarly, few of us really think through our positions before a meeting. The result is that when we speak about an issue, we are usually able to communicate only a portion of what we think and feel.

In the typical meeting, where most people are engaging in the type of content-oriented, critical listening I described above, whatever you say usually gets challenged quickly. You get cut off, then you half-listen and cut off the person who cut you off. As a result, each of you finds yourself either defending a tentative or arbitrary position or abandoning it without further consideration.

To short-circuit such frustrating interactions, it is enormously valuable to attempt to understand the person who is speaking—without judgment or argument. It helps the speaker get much clearer about what he is really trying to communicate. It helps him understand the logic behind his statements. As you ask occasional questions to better understand just what he means, he is forced to gain more clarity about his thinking on the issue in order to help you understand. As a result of this process, it is not unusual for people to completely change (or at least evolve) their positions. Conversely, common critical listening usually results in frozen positions, arguments, and ill feeling.

Listening for insight

Quiet, reflective listening—listening to allow understanding to suddenly strike you—changes the entire tone and result of a meeting. In contrast to traditional content-oriented listening, reflective listening requires a clear mind and full presence. In order to listen fully, you cannot have anything else on your mind. Again, this means no positions, no judgments, no evaluations, no comparisons, no implications or applications.

Does the deeper type of listening I've been describing in this chapter sound difficult? Most folks think so when they first read or hear about it, but they find it is quite easy when they catch on. The trick is not to consider whether you agree or disagree with what the person says. You have plenty of time later to entertain such thoughts.

The true purpose of reflective/insightful listening is to get a deeper sense of the person's world and to *make certain that the speaker feels completely understood.* The person talking gets to be the final judge of whether or not you have truly listened well. He or she will know from a certain feeling—just as you and I know whether someone has really listened to and understood us.

Unconditional respect is absolutely essential

Unconditional respect allows you to listen without judgment. Without the feeling of respect, the openness cannot be there for you to listen fully. With respect, understanding can flow.

But how can you respect someone whose opinions you don't value? Most people I talk with believe that respect must be earned. We need a different understanding about respect in this case.

Unconditional respect means that whether or not you agree with another person's actions, statements, and positions, you have a feeling of unconditional regard for that person as a fellow human being. At the very least, you feel neutral toward the person and are curious to hear and understand what he or she has to say. This feeling of respect is immediately evident to the speaker. And when you are unable to find that respect, the other person senses that too.

A good example of how we sense the presence or absence of respect is when we visit a physician. Many physicians are so busy (mentally as well as physically) that they are barely present when they meet with us. As a result, the patient feels that the doctor did not spend enough time to be really helpful. The patient will not feel respect. In contrast, I have seen physicians who spend less time but are so present and undistracted that their patients feel well cared for. Because these patients sense respect from their doctors, they say that their doctors spent all the time in the world with them.

When listening gets impaired

As you listen to someone, you may find yourself falling into reaction, judgment, and agreement/ disagreement. The moment you catch yourself doing this, just stop it! (Believe it or not, you and I *are* in control of our thinking.) You need only remember that such mental activity is not appropriate at the moment—it takes away from your capacity for deeper understanding and reflective listening.

Rapport

One of the great delights and rewards of insightful, reflective listening is the human connection both parties feel in the conversation experience. Another is that you get a glimpse into the other person's world. Each and every human being thinks about, sees, and experiences life in a unique way—a separate reality. Fully listening to another person is like a trip to a foreign country. The values, views, morals, ethics, and opinions of that person will be like no other. (It is challenging to stay neutral and not fall into judgment.) As you listen fully, with nothing on your mind, you will begin to gain an understanding, if not an appreciation, for the other person's worldview.

Remember that it is not difficult to listen this way. It is the most natural thing in the world. In fact, we have had to learn to listen critically. We have picked up mental habits such as being distracted; young children do not start out that way. They naturally listen with high presence and no distractions.

Critical listening vs. deep reflective listening

Here are two scenarios of a discussion in a meeting. The first is the common situation where content-oriented or critical listening reigns. The second is a repeat with deep reflective listening.

The Usual

Department Manager
Look, it just isn't possible for us to cut back our people by 10%. I understand that we are facing some hard money times, but my department is already lean.

CEO (Impatient and distracted)
Everybody faces the same problem. We are not picking on you specifically. We have run the numbers and the only way we can get back to profitability is to cut overhead 10% across the board!

Department manager
I know that. But you are penalizing me because I run a lean operation in the first place. If I had played the game like everyone else and padded my department, then I could cut 10% with no problem. But if I cut people now, we won't be able to do our job. I feel....

CEO (Cutting him off)
We can't stop doing our jobs. We'll all just have to work a little harder to make it happen. We're all in the same boat. I imagine everyone here feels they run a lean operation and that they will suffer hardship too.

Department Manager
I'm not trying to be difficult, but I know that you will not be happy with upset customers when we can't take care of them on time.

CEO
Well, you and everyone else will just have to make it work.

In this scenario, the manager will go away with ill feelings and unnecessary impediments in implementing the needed changes.

Now let's play this scene again, but imagine that the CEO has shifted into quiet, reflective listening. Remember her purpose is to thoroughly understand the person speaking and to have the speaker feel understood.

The Ideal

Department Manager
Look, it just isn't possible for us to cut back our people by 10%. I understand that we are facing some hard money times, but my department is already lean.

CEO (Respectfully listening—wanting to understand)
Tell me more about that.

Department Manager
Well, we are already pressed to do our work with the people we have. I cannot imagine taking care of customers the way we are supposed to with 10% fewer people.

CEO
I see. So you feel that you are already as efficient and lean as it is possible to operate effectively. You are concerned that cutting 10% would incapacitate your operation. Is that right?

Department Manager
That's about it. I mean, I suppose there is always room for improvement, but I can't imagine 10%. Besides it's not just the number of people. It's the ability to cover and be responsive.

CEO
What do you mean by ability to cover?

Department manager
Well, we have to cover 16 hours a day. So it's not as though you just arbitrarily decide not to answer 10% of the calls.

CEO
I really want to understand this. You are the Department Manager and know your area better than I do. But what you are saying just doesn't quite make sense to me. I have a hunch there is more to this than what you are saying. What's really bothering you about this?

Department Manager
Well, all of my people have been with me for years. How can I fire any of them? These aren't just numbers on a page, these are people with families who depend on their jobs. And they have been loyal to us over the years. It just isn't right.

CEO
Now *that* I think we can all identify with. I hate having to lay anybody off. But unless this group can come up with a way to cut 10% of our overhead without laying off people, or significantly increasing revenues, I don't see any other choice.

Department manager
Hmm. I guess you're right. Maybe we can find another way.

This time the manager will leave the meeting focused on finding workable solutions rather than focused on ill feelings. He may not be too happy with the economic situation but he knows that he was listened to and understood.

Insightful listening leverages time

Once a person feels fully understood, he has little need to keep expounding on the same issue. At that point, he is more open to considering other views. As clients begin to learn about reflective, deep listening, they sometimes feel that it takes too much time. It does take longer to listen reflectively and to truly understand. It often takes several attempts to truly understand the world of the speaker and to be able to articulate it to the speaker's satisfaction. But, in my experience, any time invested in listening is more than compensated for by the ease with which everything moves ahead more efficiently later on.

As the leader trying to get someone to do something, think about how many times you have had to go back and repeat or clarify because your communication was mainly one-sided. You did not take the time to make certain that the other person actually understood your communication and that you understood what problems she might have with what you are asking her to do.

As the person being talked to, you know that it is much more difficult to buy into someone else's position or directives—even the boss's—when you don't feel that your point of view is understood. There is that nagging feeling that if you had only been able to make him understand.... As a result, if you don't feel you were respectfully listened to and understood, you will usually drag your feet in carrying out the action, which serves neither you nor your boss. Remember that the measure of whether the other person is listening respectfully and truly hearing you is not whether she agrees with you in the end. It is in the feeling you have of truly being understood.

When the speaker feels understood, there is little need for that person to keep repeating the same message in various ways—or more adamantly. This significantly reduces meeting time.

Reading this book

In reading this book, I suggest you take a similar approach to what I have described here for insightful, reflective listening. Don't study it or focus on content. The value here is insight and deeper understanding. Understanding will strike you more often if you are reading reflectively. Don't study it or try to figure anything out. Just cruise along (some people call it the "novel mode," as in pleasure reading) and trust that understanding will come to you if you stay open-minded and keep it light.

Summing up

Reflective or insightful listening leads to a feeling of common humanity and mutual understanding. It quiets the speaker's thinking and helps him to see what he is saying with more clarity. This listening opens the door for the speaker to consider, in turn, what you have to say. This respectful exchange dramatically shortens meeting time. Reflective listening is one of two key tools (along with tone management that we will cover later) in the wise stewardship of any meeting. It is quite natural. In fact, the only things that interfere with reflective listening are our habitual mental habits: judgment, analysis, comparison, preoccupation, distracted wandering, and thinking we already know what the person means. This same approach of dropping the mental habits applies equally to reading this book for insights.

It takes two to speak the truth—one to speak, and another to hear.

—**Henry David Thoreau**

Coming up...

In the next chapter, we will explore states of mind and how to optimize meetings by guiding and influencing the quality of thinking.

3

HIGH-PERFORMANCE
STATES
From Grace to the Zone

The zone is a transcendent state of mind that human beings sometimes access, resulting in extraordinary performance and intense levels of enjoyment. It is part of our natural, healthy range of thinking. While hitting the zone may not happen every day, attaining healthier, higher-quality states of mind is quite easy.

We read about it all the time. Artists get so carried away with their painting or sculpture that they neglect sleep and food. Writers get into a stream of consciousness where it feels like the book is writing itself. Athletes find themselves playing beyond anything they ever thought possible—and most of it seems to happen in slow motion. They speak of this phenomenon as "elasticity of time." Seconds seem like hours, hours seem like minutes.

Several decades ago, the psychologist Mihaly Csikszentmihalyi studied why so many creative people experienced such depths of enjoyment and heightened rushes of creativity. He called the state of mind "flow." In 1990 he published *Flow: The Psychology of Optimal Experience*. In his work, Csikszentmihalyi interviewed hundreds of people who experienced flow in numerous professions, in cultures all over the world. He found this state occurring in athletes, artists, writers, musicians, Japanese motorcycle-gang members, Navajo shepherds, assembly-line workers in Chicago, surgeons, and others. All of these people reported experiences of deep joy, total immersion, light spirits, heightened sense of mastery, lack of self-consciousness, and self-transcendence.

In the field of athletics, we hear frequent stories about extraordinary events athletes have experienced. In an interview, Bill Russell was reminiscing about the most incredible basketball game of his career. Russell said that both teams were in the zone the entire game. Every player was playing the best basketball of his life and bringing out the best in every other player. By the end of the game, no one cared about the final score. All that mattered was that they had been catapulted to levels of performance and joy they had rarely experienced before.

High states of mind are innate

There is nothing mysterious about these high states of mind. Children under the age of five live a great deal of their lives in or near this state. They experience indiscriminate enjoyment in just about every moment of their lives—even with the simplest things. If the source of their joy were circumstantial (contingent on what they did or where they were), then we would all find joy in the same things. Not so.

The source of this joy is connected to our wise use of our thought process and our state of mind.

I rarely meet someone who has not experienced that heightened state, or something close to it. Sometimes it happens when listening to or playing music, sometimes when engaging in a sport, sometimes when sitting by a stream in the woods or on the beach, sometimes in deep conversation with a close friend. Actually it can happen under any circumstance while fully engaged in any activity.

High-state meetings? Once in a while, I run into someone who says that they experienced something like that in a meeting. I know that I have, but it is not so common.

I am not suggesting that every meeting will take place at an extraordinary high-state level. Depending on how we use our ability to think, there are infinite possibilities. We all have an innate, high-performance mental continuum that ranges from contentment to an exultant sense of effortless mastery. My experience is that when people in a meeting are at least within the high-performance continuum, the meetings will be most effective and rewarding. (See Figure 3-1.)

One of the most natural and easily attained functional levels of this healthy-thinking continuum is characterized by effortless grace. You don't have to be inspired or enthralled; just imagine a meeting that flows effortlessly. Even that would be a vast improvement over most business meetings these days.

MEETING LEVELS

STATE OF MIND	MEETING IMPACT
Zone, flow	Magic
Genius	Visionary
Creative	Solutions
Insightful	Efficient, effective
Effortless, graceful	Smooth flow
At ease, present	Alert, focused

HEALTHY ↑ THOUGHT
UNHEALTHY ↓ THOUGHT

Stressed, pressured	Tension
Worried, preoccupied	Scattered
Disgruntled, unhappy	Inhibiting
Fearful, insecure	Divisive
Upset, angry	Disruptive
Discouraged, depressed	Lead blanket

Figure 3-1

At this point, you may be asking, "Just how much of what we are discussing does everyone in the meeting need to know in order to impact the meeting positively?" The answer is, the more the better, which is why managers give their employees books like this to digest. But even if you are the only one in the meeting who understands the principles about thinking and state of mind, your level of healthy understanding can have a major, positive influence on any meeting. We will talk about this in more depth in the chapter 19.

Summing up

Effective meetings depend on participants who are operating in higher, healthier states of mind that lead to effortless, graceful interaction. Sometimes these states soar to extraordinary levels that we call the groove, the zone, or flow. But even when we have not reached extraordinary levels, it is natural for us to operate with centered, healthy thinking that produces great results with minimal effort. We were born with this capacity.

Not everything that counts can be counted, and not everything that can be counted counts.
—**Albert Einstein**

Coming up...

We need only understand a few simple principles to reclaim our birthright of operating in a high-performance state of mind. In the next chapter, we will begin to discuss those principles.

4

WHAT GOES ON
BETWEEN THE EARS
A Peek Under the Hood

Understanding the role of Thought in the human experience is essential to leading highly effective meetings. Understanding what opens and closes people's minds, how to tap creativity, how to empower good decision-making, and how to foster healthy relationships—in other words, understanding the human factor—is the understanding you'll need on the road to high-performance meetings.

Early in my 13-year industrial career, when I was managing process engineering, manufacturing, or quality assurance in a high-tech operation, several questions kept tugging at me:

Why are some people easy to work with and others quite difficult? Why is it that one day I can communicate delicate information so that people accept it well, and on other days no matter how cautious I am, people react negatively to whatever I say?

Why do I feel creative and capable some days, and at other times, absolutely uninspired?

What did it mean when a friendly colleague confided that no matter how nicely I talked, he always felt wrong at the end of a conversation?

Why do I react so strongly to certain situations or people—usually the same types?

Why are some people self-motivated, while others have to be prodded constantly?

Why is it that I can be totally stumped about a tough problem, and then have the solution appear when I least expect it?

How could a colleague say I wasn't listening when I could repeat what he said verbatim?

Why do some meetings drag while others seem to fly?

Yes, I was certainly full of questions!

The journey I started back then has taken me to some amazing experiences and resources. But despite some dead ends and rough roads along the way, a commonsense understanding has evolved over the years that makes the answers to all of these questions—and many more—quite obvious.

By the end of this chapter, you will have begun to answer some of these questions for yourself and deepened your understanding about the human factor. As a natural result, the way you live and work, including how you conduct meetings, will begin to improve and evolve. Understanding is highly leveraged.

State of mind

In any meeting the better (healthier) the state of mind of the participants, the higher the quality of the meeting. But what is "state of mind" exactly? State of mind is the overall quality of a person's thinking at any moment. Everyone's quality of thinking, and thus everyone's state of mind, fluctuates throughout the day. These fluctuations in the quality of thinking are what we call moods. It turns out that the more a person understands that moods are a natural result of the shifting quality of *his or her own* thinking, the less severe are these fluctuations. In fact, deeper understanding always leads to an overall improved quality of thinking—which means higher states of mind. It is quite common for people who have gained this deeper understanding to report that they still have mood swings but that the extremes are no longer there.

When someone does not understand that moods are a natural result of the shifting quality of *their* own thinking, then it appears that the world is changing out there. Here is a practical example to illustrate how this process works. The boss announces that sales must pick up or else. Both Ann and Mary think "Or else what?" Both wonder, "Does that mean I may lose my job?" Then Ann's and Mary's thinking go in quite different directions. Driven by insecure thinking, Ann's next thought is "What will happen if I lose my job? Will I be able to find another? Times are tough in this business. Will I lose my house?" As a result of this continuing downward spiral of thinking, Ann experiences increasing fear and may drop into a low mood where she becomes much less effective as her state of mind reaches lower levels.

Mary, on the other hand, catches the beginning feelings of insecurity that accompany the thought, "Does that mean I may lose my job?" Her level of understanding is somewhat deeper than Ann's; in other words, she realizes more about the connection between Thought and experience than Ann does. Therefore, Mary immediately dismisses the thought of losing her job, because she knows where it will lead. Her next thought is "Well, the boss means business, so I guess I'd better get to it." Her level of understanding about her think-ing and *the fact that she knows she is doing the thinking,* rather than being a victim of outside circumstances, is what pro-tects her. That understanding allows her to drop the fright-ening thoughts that otherwise would likely spiral into a self-fulfilling prophecy of failure. It provides her with a more philosophical perspective and the opportunity to create a totally different experience and result simply by the way she uses her powers of Thought.

The very fact that Mary short-circuits her negative think-ing is what heads her in a more positive, proactive, and pro-ductive direction. As her state of mind naturally becomes more positive, she begins to see more solutions, more possi-bilities, and more opportunities. In contrast, Ann sees fewer and fewer solutions. Storm clouds of insecure thinking have overcome her. Ironically, she does not realize that she ulti-mately controls the weather of her thinking.

Understanding the building blocks of the human experience

Without dragging you through endless details and mean-ingless psychobabble, I would like to lay out a practical and powerful understanding about people. Had I known even a fraction of this in my earlier years, I would have been a far more effective leader. My meetings might have been closer to the zone instead of the doldrums.

How we create our experience

To run effective meetings and manage successful relation-ships, it is important to understand how each person creates his or her individual experience and personal reality from moment to moment. In my work with clients, I find that as soon as people begin to grasp how this process works, they immediately improve their effectiveness in every aspect on the job—and at home. That is, they naturally start to operate in more effective states of mind.

Three principles determine how we function psychologically. In brief form, these are:

Thought

Thought is the power to change our experience of life. As long as we are alive, we are always thinking. As a matter of survival, every human being is born knowing how to use the power of Thought in a creative, positive, life-affirming manner. I will refer to this positive use of Thought as our innate psychological health or innate health. It is similar to the immune system, which is designed to keep our bodies physically healthy. In this innate, healthy use of the power of Thought, thoughts as content stream through our head like water flowing down a river. If a negative or disturbing thought occurs to us, we notice it but naturally let it float on downstream. When we lose our bearings and get lost in acquired, unproductive thought habits, such as stress, speeded-up thinking, worry, ruminating, and judging, thoughts churn and erode our sense of well-being.

Consciousness

Consciousness is the is the ability to be aware of creation—how we create our unique experience of life. The resulting sensory phenomena are what we experience and call "reality." More accurately, we should call reality our *personal reality* or *personal experience,* since it comes from our *personal* thinking and is like no other's reality.

When a person begins to recognize that he or she is the thinker (creator) of his or her personal reality via the power of Thought, a major shift occurs. We will talk more about this later.

Mind

Mind is the universal creative energy that powers Thought and Consciousness. Mind, as I am using the term, does not refer to our brain, but rather the power source behind everything—the creative energy of the universe. Mind is the source of creativity, new ideas, brilliant solutions—everything. Different people have different names for this creative energy. However, names are not the point of this discussion. Realizing that such a source exists and is available to us is the point. This is not a religious or philosophic issue. It is a matter of looking at what is so and how this all works.

Now let's put these three principles together and see how they are at work within each of us at every moment. Mind powers Thought and Consciousness. Whatever thought I entertain becomes alive and real for me by Consciousness via my five senses.

↗ CONSCIOUSNESS

MIND   **⇨ PERSONAL REALITY**

↘ THOUGHT

What this means is that whatever you and I are thinking becomes our experience—instantly. Conversely, **everything we experience *must* come from the way we use or misuse the power of Thought!** The powers of Thought and Consciousness are neutral. Only the content of our thinking determines the quality of our experience. To say it another way, the powers of Thought and Consciousness have no position or stake. Whatever thought—positive or negative—we entertain becomes our personal experience in that moment.

These principles have always been alive in the world. Sydney Banks, author of many books and audio/video programs, articulated these principles in the early 1970's.

Do I really need to understand this stuff?

Well, yes, you do to some extent, if you hope to be able to guide your meetings toward high performance and enjoyment. The more you understand it, the more effective you will be at work, in meetings, and in all relationships. Or to say it another way, the deeper your understanding of these three principles and the deeper your realization that you are the thinker, the more powerful an influence you become in guiding those around you toward healthier functioning and better results. This understanding keeps you "bullet proof" so that you don't take things personally. It also tends to draw others toward higher-quality thinking.

Everything starts with Thought

The DVD provides a good metaphor for the human process. A laser beam strikes the DVD disk, activating stored information. The resulting signals are processed through a receiver/amplifier to produce visual images and surround sound. In the human system, Mind is the universal energy (laser). Thought is the source of information (DVD). Consciousness is the means (receiver/amplifier) that brings it all to life. Like the DVD, all three are necessary to produce experience. In either system, eliminate one component and there is no personal experience.

Here is a simple example. I was towing a load of old power-line poles (yes we do stuff like that here in the mountains of Northern California). The rig jack knifed and rolled over. As I hung upside down from my seat belt with the roof caved into the steering wheel, my single thought was to get out. The only sound I heard was gasoline leaking from the tank. Fortunately, my wife and I were able to release ourselves and crawl out through an open window. Driven by embarrassment, I immediately began unloading the trailer to clear the highway—hoping no one would ever find out what I had done. A half hour later when friends came by to help clear the highway, one of them pointed out a gash in my arm. Up to that point I had no experience of pain because I had no thought for it—until they pointed it out! Prior to that moment, my thinking had been occupied with unloading poles and cleaning up the mess. The moment I noticed the gash, my thoughts were on the injury, and my senses brought that thought to life (Consciousness) through the pain.

Here is a similar example. I have heard that when medics ran out of morphine in Vietnam, they injected saline solution and told the suffering it was morphine. Just as many people found relief from the saline as from the morphine. We call this a placebo effect. This is neither magic nor mystery? Once again Thought and Consciousness are creating personal reality.

My goal in presenting these examples is to help you develop an understanding of how we human beings function so that you are better able to manage critical states of mind in meetings and relationships. What follows are three additional helpful pieces to the puzzle of human experience.

Free will

Free will is our capacity to use Thought in any way we choose—constructively or destructively. We are free to use the power of Thought in a positive way to promote creativity, enjoyment, productivity, growth, evolution, and success. We are equally free to use this power to harm others or ourselves. Thought is quite neutral; it follows our directions. So, if Thought is the steering wheel of experience, then free will is the hand on the wheel. Just realizing that your personal life experience is not "out there," but happening inside your head via Thought and Consciousness, is both liberating and empowering.

Here is an example of how one client (I will call him Bill) exercised his free will and changed the course of his life. When Bill was promoted to Department Manager, he apparently decided that he had to prove himself and "act like a boss." Over the next year or so, Bill became increasingly insensitive to people; in fact, he became a tyrant. He found himself stressed and angry much of the time, and his employees were becoming dissatisfied with his treatment. I was brought in to help Bill find his bearings and return to the world of human beings. As we worked together, Bill realized that all the pressure, stress, and threats he perceived in his work environment were all made up in his own thinking. He realized that it was not only possible, but also more effective, to work in a centered state and bring compassion and understanding as well as firmness to the people he managed and coached. Using his free will, Bill simply stopped entertaining the thoughts that led him away from common sense and wisdom. Instead, he began to go with those thoughts that felt right in his centered state of mind. Within days, Bill was feeling more secure and healthy, and the job looked quite different to him. Everyone noticed the change—including his family. By taking responsibility for his own thinking, Bill used his free will to change the course of his life.

Level of understanding

The depth to which you and I recognize and understand how all of this works is called our *level of understanding*. Sometimes you will hear people speak of level of consciousness. It means the same thing—your level of conscious understanding of the principles. This level of understanding is the extent to which *you realize that you are the one doing the thinking and creating your experience of life from moment to moment*. Realizing this simple fact eliminates virtually all feelings of being victimized and powerless. You begin to recognize that it is not what happens "out there" that determines how you feel and what you experience, but rather what you make out of circumstances via your use of Thought. Remember Dirty Harry's famous line "Make my day?" Well, you and I do just that. It's not what happens out there in life—it's what we make of it with our thinking.

Keeping on track—the compass of feelings

None of us can objectively evaluate our own thinking because we are like fish in water about it. If you ask yourself the question, "Is my judgment right on this matter," the logic that prompted the decision will self-validate. Like the fund managers who invested in derivatives and were caught in rapidly changing interest rates, "it seemed like a good idea at the time." When we make decisions, they make sense at the time based on the quality of logic (state of mind) and data available at that moment. On another day, in a higher state of mind, and with a higher quality of thinking available, the situation may look different—leaving you wondering how you could have thought it made sense back then. Yet it did.

Thought-quality control relies on a feeling. But remember, every experience (even a feeling) starts with a thought. Therefore, *the key is to become increasingly aware of your feeling state, because that is the only clue you will have about the quality of your thinking available at that moment*. I realize that men very often hide or deny feelings—especially the subtle ones. However, ignoring feelings in guiding your use of Thought would be like ignoring your sense of balance when riding a bicycle.

For example, suppose you have just come back from a meeting with your boss. You are upset because your request for special equipment has been denied; the funds were allocated to another department. As you walk into your office, one of your employees greets you with a problem he is having with an uncooperative colleague. Your first thought (reaction) is to tell him to "Handle it!" because his problem seems like small potatoes compared with what has just happened to your new equipment. If you don't pay attention to your feelings (in this case, a feeling of being upset—perhaps angry), you're likely to snap out some reply that you will later regret. But if you are paying attention to your compass of feelings, you will realize that your quality of thought (state of mind) is not the best right now. You might suggest a later meeting when you have had a chance to cool down.

Low-quality thinking is characterized by feelings of burden, apathy, discouragement, upset, anger, envy, resentment, irritation, embarrassment, and similar negative feelings. Higher-quality thinking characteristically brings feelings of hope, inspiration, aliveness, creativity, warmth, humor, and compassion. So staying tuned into your feeling state gives you a reliable indicator about the quality of your thinking. Remember, every feeling or emotion we have starts with Thought. Feelings are our built-in compass for the quality of our thinking at any moment. The good news is that a healthy use of Thought is something we were born with.

Common sense dictates that if you are in a state of low-quality thinking, you should be wary and make as few decisions as possible. Don't decide that this is the time to get into a discussion with a difficult employee, child, or mate. You just have to find the humility to realize that when you are in a state of low-quality thinking, you are probably not seeing things with perspective and wisdom.

If you don't like how you are feeling, use your free will to stop entertaining the troubling thoughts and clear your head. This is as simple as letting go and relaxing into a centered state. That will allow you to return to your innate, healthy state of mind where you are more at ease, responsive, graceful, and effective. I know what I am saying sounds like it is easier said than done, so here are some tips:

- Focus on becoming more aware of when you are having troubling thoughts or falling into dysfunctional habits of thinking (worry, judgment, busy-mindedness).

- Lower your tolerance for dysfunctional thoughts.

- Set your sights on moving away from low-quality thinking and toward a healthier use of Thought.

As you become more aware of your dysfunctional thinking habits, they will become louder and more obvious in your head. For example, if you are worried or speedy-minded, you will start to feel like you are constantly worrying about something or that your world is spinning much too fast. Nothing has changed; you are just noticing a mental habit. In a way, this new awareness works just like your body's immune system. As the habit becomes more obvious, your innate health will steer you away from the habit back toward a healthier, more centered state of mind—the default setting for human beings. We steer naturally toward health.

In a state of higher-quality thinking, your feeling state may vary from feelings of contentment to feelings of inspiration and exhilaration. You will tend to see things from a wiser perspective when you are in higher states of mind. Decisions made from this healthier, wiser state of mind tend to work out better. Not that you won't make mistakes, but you can generally trust your thinking when your feeling compass tells you that you are accessing higher-quality thinking.

It should be obvious at this point that meetings have varying qualities of thinking as well. The thinking quality of a meeting is simply the cumulative thinking quality of the participants. For example, some meetings inspire and bring out the best use of Thought. In such meetings, everyone feels like a genius. Other meetings end up grinding away from topic to topic, resulting in little creativity or inspiration. In those meetings, participants end up feeling dull, tired and wasted.

We, as individuals, can be operating along a broad continuum from fearful, dysfunctional thinking to constructive, inspired thinking. As with all uses of Thought, these qualities of individual thinking express themselves as a group average or collective feeling in the meeting. We call this collective quality of thought the **tone of the meeting**. The more healthy and high-functioning people there are in the meeting, the higher the meeting tone. The higher the meeting tone, the more productive the meeting and the more satisfying the experience for participants. Anyone can recognize the tone change in a meeting: grinding, fatiguing, boring, interesting, inspiring, fun, exhilarating. It's just that not too many people know what to do when the meeting heads down the sewer. We'll address this question in greater detail in a later chapter.

Summing up

We have been given the extraordinary gifts of Mind, Thought and Consciousness which allow us to create our unique personal experience or reality moment to moment. We have also been given the gift of realizing that we are doing the creating from moment to moment, via the power of Thought. As each of us recognizes at more profound levels that we are the thinker (architect) of this event called "my reality," we find greater ease and enjoyment in every aspect of life. By paying attention to our feelings and emotions, we can monitor how well we are using the gift of Thought at any given moment. We are born with a healthy use of Thought. We return to this natural state when we stop pulling ourselves away from it with our learned, dysfunctional habits of thinking. This basic understanding will make you more effective in running high-toned meetings.

"Mind, Consciousness and Thought are the three principles that enable us to acknowledge and respond to existence.

All human behavior and social structures on earth are formed via Mind, Consciousness and Thought."

—**Sydney Banks**

Coming up...

In Chapter 5, we will examine typical thinking that is often invisible to us but nevertheless shapes our view of life and our personal realities.

NOTES & REMINDERS

The mind is not a vessel to be filled but a fire to be kindled.

Plutarch

5

WE ARE FISH IN WATER
Invisible Influences

Much of our thinking (assumptions, beliefs) is invisible to us. Nevertheless, it conditions and often limits our view and experience of life.

Fish are probably not aware that they live in a reality of water. It is essentially invisible to fish. Fish just accept as unquestioned fact that they float and move as they wriggle their fins and bodies. We, like fish, swim in a reality of which most of us are unaware. Our personal reality is made of Thought. What we see, hear, smell, feel, and taste depends on Thought. Deep understanding of this fact is immensely helpful in guiding meetings successfully.

Thought is THE critical element in how we see and experience life. This is true whether or not we are conscious of our thoughts, just as it is true that the fish swims in water whether or not it recognizes that it does.

Thought: the architect of "realities"

The following is what I call our Thought-Reality Cycle. Remember that every part of this cycle is Thought.

THOUGHT - REALITY CYCLE

Thought
(Conclusion) (Belief/Assumption)

↗   ↘
Conclusion   Feeling
↑   ↓

State of Mind
Result   (quality of thinking)
↖   Behavior   ↙
(Action/inaction)

Figure 5-1

Limiting self-concept

Let's look at a simple example of this cycle in action. A young student with underdeveloped motor skills overhears a comment from the teacher that he has no talent for drawing. He concludes, "I can't draw" (thought). At the next drawing assignment, up pops the thought, "I can't draw." Perhaps the child feels discouraged or resigned (feeling), and this leads to a lower state of mind. He consequently makes little effort to draw well or improve (behavior). After all, what's the use—"I can't draw anyway." The result is another poor drawing, which reinforces the original thought. "I can't draw" is continually reinforced and becomes an unquestioned reality (thought) for that child.

In an assignment to resolve interdepartmental conflicts, I found this cycle at work. During assessment interviews, all fingers pointed to one supervisor—let's call him John.

According to most reports, John was a troublemaker who simply would not cooperate. In talking with John, I discovered that all the parties had formerly worked together as one department. The problem started when John's manager set up a new department and made John a supervisor. The original department felt threatened by the change and treated new supervisor John with cold suspicion—apparently fearing that the new department posed a threat in competing for resources.

When John encountered this initial resistance, he concluded (thought) that people in the original department didn't like him anymore. This thought led to his feeling tense, upset, and defensive when around them (feeling). As a result, John's state of mind dropped. John's defensive reaction (behavior) was to overcompensate and demand what he needed. His demanding attitude triggered bad feelings and resistance (result) in the people he dealt with. Their mounting unwillingness to cooperate and their unfriendly attitudes only justified and reinforced their thoughts that he posed a threat. For months, this cycle continued to reinforce and forge a "reality" in which the two departments could not work together. Everyone saw these behaviors and attitudes as "reality."

Fortunately, as I worked with him, John soon realized what had happened. He recognized that he had been hoodwinked by his own thinking. *At that moment of realization,* he broke the old cycle. He even understood why his colleagues were behaving the way they did—and that it would not change overnight. His attitude changed around the other department, and eventually their reactions changed. Relations between the departments soon smoothed out. A new cooperative reality was built—via Thought.

It is worth emphasizing the point about John's realization. It was not information alone that worked in this case. John managed to get reflective long enough to have a blinding flash of the obvious. He stopped being defensive and was able to step back and take a fresh look. He was able to see his thoughts as the architect of his reality. Thus, his thinking evolved and his changed behavior followed. And so did his changed reality.

Reinforcing success

The same Thought-Reality Cycle that set off John's problems at work can operate in a positive direction as well. A woman new to sales finds her first sales call enjoyable—even though she did not make the sale. Her conclusion (thought) is that sales calls are not as difficult as people had told her they would be; in fact they are enjoyable. Before the next sales call, the woman has the same thought, and she experiences eager anticipation (feeling). As a result of her positive feelings and engaging manner, she instinctively creates a relaxed, open environment with the prospect (behavior). The prospect becomes interested in her products and commits to a small order (result). Her conclusion (thought) is that selling is not so difficult, and indeed is enjoyable. And so the cycle continues. At some point, she will see that sometimes you make the sale and sometimes you do not. But each sales call can be an enjoyable experience for her and her prospect.

Recognizing that personal reality is always Thought

Just recognizing that Thought continually weaves the tapestry of our reality and that we are the thinker allows us to avoid taking our own thinking too seriously. For example, realizing that "I'm no good and will never amount to anything" is just a thought (memory or belief) allows us to move beyond the limitation of self-deprecating thoughts. Such thoughts erode our natural sense of well-being and result in what we call low self-esteem. (Yes, even low self-esteem is just thought.) Without this understanding, such thoughts become "givens" in our lives and are rarely examined or challenged. A circumstance becomes "just the way it is."

Thought in disguise

It's helpful to recognize various kinds of thought as they create what we call our life, reality, or worldview. Being able to recognize thought helps us enjoy successful relationships, find ease in the workplace, and guide successful meetings. Figure 5-2 is a sample grouping of some common types of thoughts, and how people generally recognize them in day-to-day living.

LEVELS OF THOUGHT RECOGNITION

Just my thoughts

- Pipe dreams
- Nightmares
- Fantasy,
- Information
- some memories
- bizarre ideas

My worldview

- Ethics
- Values
- Morals
- Opinions

"Reality—the way it is"

- Unrecognized thought
- Basic assumptions
- Givens
- Conclusions from experiences
- Unquestioned beliefs
- Conditions

↑ M O R E

R E C O G N I T I O N

L E S S ↓

Figure 5-2

The way we see and respond to each level is quite different. For example, in the top group, **Just My Thoughts**, most of us recognize these as just thoughts that occur to us. Someone might fantasize that she won the lottery, but few people run around spending their winnings based on the thought. Waking up from a nightmare means that you shift from living in its terror while you are asleep to recognizing that it was just a bad dream—also just thought. If challenged about thoughts in the top category, most of us would acknowledge that they are just our thoughts and ideas, certainly not worth arguing about or defending.

In the group of less recognized thoughts, which I'm calling **My Worldview**, we hold thoughts more dear. Through training, experience, and reflection, we generate a set of thoughts about our conduct of life. Examples are whether we should live by the rules of society, how we should treat others, whether we should be truthful. Since the thoughts in this group tend to guide our daily living, we don't tend to recognize them as thoughts quite as readily as the thoughts in the first group. Yet if pressed, most people will admit eventually that these too are thoughts. However, when our thinking at this level is challenged, most of us are quick to defend these thoughts. In most cases, we have accumulated a strong base of underlying logic to justify these thoughts—our values and morals.

At the least recognized level of Thought, which I'm calling **Reality**, our thoughts are essentially unquestioned. We are truly like fish in water. That is, we take things for granted and seldom recognize the thoughts in this group as thought. For example, before the mid 1950's, runners took for granted that it was not possible to run a mile faster than four minutes. Scientific papers had been published showing how the physiology of the human body precluded faster times. However, Roger Bannister reasoned that if he could run a quarter mile in less than a minute, then he could run four in a row to break that barrier. His breakthrough was carried in just about every paper in the world. The week following his famous new record, many college and even some high-school students across the country also broke the four-minute mile. It was not possible before only because that "reality" of impossibility was held via thought.

Here is another example of how Thought can seem like unquestionable reality. A bodybuilder once told a colleague and me that weightlifters think they "know" their weight limits. As a spotter, he has told a lifter that there was 250 pounds on the bar—that lifter's current limit, when in fact he had loaded 300 pounds. The lifter had no trouble pressing it. But when told it was, in fact, 300 pounds, the man could no longer lift it.

At this level of Thought, we seldom question things because we take for granted that "This is the way it is." This is simply "reality." Until we recognize Thought as thought rather than absolute reality, we are literally bound in an invisible cage of our own making. When challenged at this level, most of us will vehemently defend our thoughts. In fact, this level of Thought is where wars start. Sometimes people are willing to die for the "reality" they see. They will argue and fight to defend "the way it is." Countless religious wars are tragic examples of this.

To each his own

Every human being's thinking is unique—a separate reality. Therefore, what each of us calls "the way it is" is unique. No person's reality is more "true" than any other. In that sense, my reality is true for me, just as your reality is true for you. Understanding this essential fact is a great help in resolving and avoiding conflict. Acrimonious arguments, battles, and wars are the result of people not understanding how Thought is connected to individual perception and reality. This lack of understanding often creates havoc in meetings. Therefore, it is important to realize that each of us is creating and sustaining our personal, separate reality using our unique thinking.

Summing up

Everything we experience via our five senses starts with Thought. There is nothing "out there" that makes us feel a certain way. How we feel is only what we make of outside circumstances with our use of Thought. Once we realize that everything begins and ends with our own thoughts, we can choose to break the Thought- Reality Cycle by simply changing our thinking.

Thought is so powerful and pervasive that we can unwittingly think ourselves into cages of limitation, but we can also use Thought as a launching site for new possibilities at every moment. The choice is ours.

Recognizing Thought as THE active agent in the human experience provides us with perspective on our reality and others' realities. Realizing that each of us is the thinker of our own reality helps us remember the total relativity of "the way it is."

Understanding the role of Thought in human behavior helps all of us see other people's behavior in a more understanding light. After all, it is all just Thought and we are the thinkers. The deeper you understand the role of Thought as the architect of human experience, the easier it is to guide the interactions of people in meetings to higher levels of effectiveness. Keep your eye on thought and state of mind, not behavior.

Sometimes my eyes make up things. Sometimes I see what I want to see.

—Charlie Kausen, age 5 (yep, my grandson)

Coming up...

In the next chapter we will talk about our birthright of resiliency. You will see that guiding your thinking away from limitations and toward creativity and higher states of mind is easier done than said.

6

INNATE HEALTH, COMMON SENSE, AND CREATIVITY
It's all natural

Each of us is born with a naturally healthy use of Thought. We are creative, resourceful, fast learning, imaginative, and often uncommonly wise. Anything to the contrary is misused Thought—a learned mental habit or self-limiting beliefs and memories.

In many meetings, you might doubt that anyone can operate in a sensible, wise manner. The healthy states of mind that we have been discussing would appear to have been checked at the door. Consequently, any hope of moving a meeting to more effective levels seems remote. The hopeful news is that healthy levels of mental functioning are always there waiting to come back. Let's look further.

Buoyant health

Each of us is born with an inherently healthy use of thought—innate health. It is how we learn, adapt, and grow as human beings. This is not something we have to learn or discover. It is one of our most basic capacities from birth. Simply stated, we just need to do our best not to override our innate mental health in ways that drag us down to lower-quality levels of mental functioning. At lower levels we become reactive and make poorer choices in life.

Innate mental well-being is a buoyant force in everyone. Imagine you are floating on an air mattress in a pool. Someone walks by and tosses you a 20-pound weight. (Mentally, this is like starting to worry, getting into judgments, or over-analyzing.) You and your mattress settle a little further into the water. Then someone tosses you another weight. (More serious concerns, more things are on your mind.) The mattress settles even lower in the water. As this process continues, at some point your mattress will fold and sink. (Mentally, your spirits are at a low level.) However, the instant you drop the weights (clear your head), you and your mattress shoot back to the surface. (Mentally, you are right back at your innate, healthy levels of functioning.)

Original Thought

One of the resources that this innate, healthy use of Thought provides is original Thought, also known as creativity. Everyone knows that they have creative insights from time to time. People who seem to have a lot of creative insights we often view as exceptional. I am suggesting that they are exceptional only in the sense that they may be among a minority of people who don't limit their access to their innate, creative resources. In a sense, they know enough to keep out of their own way. We can all do that.

There have been numerous surveys done asking people when they get their best ideas. The most common answers are during vacations, driving, showering, and hobbies like golfing, gardening, and fishing. Obviously some people have their best ideas while gardening, others while hiking, meditating, contemplating, praying, or just relaxing. The common element here is a clear, unburdened mind. People are in a state of innate healthy use of Thought—able to access creativity—the moment the mind is unburdened.

Creative back burner

Most folks have heard the term "put it on the back burner." This expression probably originates from the type of cooking in which you put soups on low heat and let them simmer for long periods. As a cook, you just let the food cook on its own; you don't turn up the heat to try and make it cook faster. As a thinker, you turn a problem or decision over to your creative intelligence. You let it simmer and wait for the solution or decision to hit you instead of trying to make it happen. When it does happen, it usually strikes you as an obvious solution. You will probably even wonder why you did not see it before.

When you turn something over to your creative back burner, you can define the parameters of acceptable solutions in any way you want. You can specify when you need the answer, cost and equipment limitations, performance characteristics, and so on. Sometimes I play a mental game as the CEO of my own little company called ME. When I come across a problem that I don't see an obvious answer to, I "call" my creative R&D department. I tell them about the problem and everything I know about it, what requirements the solution has to fulfill, even when I need an answer. When I "hang up," I stop thinking about it. Sometimes the problem will come to mind and I'll check in with R&D. Any answer? If not, I'll usually just tell R&D to call me when they get an answer. And they do—usually when I'm in the shower in the morning.

Here is an example. My wife and I wanted to add a great room onto our house. I asked several people, including two of our sons who are builders, what ideas they had about the roofline. In this snow country, we need to avoid designs that trap snow. No one had any ideas. Sometimes, I would ask visitors if they had any ideas. Finally, I decided that I would put the problem on the back burner and see what my creative resources came up with. The basic parameters were that the roof design could not trap snow and had to blend in with the original house so that it did not look like an addition. From time to time, I would look at the house and wonder…but no answers. Several months later, an idea came to me—of course, in the shower. (This must be the fountain of new ideas!) In a flash, I saw the design. I made a drawing and built a scale model. After the structural engineer did the technical design, the builder built it and we now enjoy the new room. No stress, no worry, just the willingness to not know the answer, the faith that I had the creative resources inside of me, and the patience to wait for it to come. Everyone has this innate capacity for creativity.

Having faith in the unknown

The more you trust your creative resources, and the more you use your back burner for decisions and problem solving, the better it seems to work. Maybe it is simply a matter of learning to stop the mental grinding and worry sooner, or not starting at all. Becoming comfortable in the unknown sometimes takes a lot of practice. For me, going into the unknown initially felt like jumping out of a window blindfolded—not knowing whether I was on the ground floor or in the penthouse. Also, my habit when I didn't know something had been to make up something that seemed reasonable. But that had kept me from accessing my creative resources.

These days, I find it quite natural to say to myself, "I don't know," when I don't immediately see an answer. As often as not, the next moment something occurs to me. To anyone else, it might look as though I always knew the answer or solution, but most of the time I don't. I simply have learned to stop searching my memory for answers and to go into the unknown without reservation. With practice and the faith that the power of original Thought will deliver, anyone can become quite proficient in using this wonderful gift.

Summing up

Learning to trust and rely upon the creative resources to which all of us have access will make you seem like a genius in some ways. The capacity for creative Thought is built into our system as part of our innate, healthy use of Thought. All we need to do is have faith in it, have patience, get comfortable in the unknown, stop worrying or cluttering our thinking in other ways, and wait for the answer to hit. It does work, and practice makes it easier.

Without this playing with fantasy no creative work has ever yet come to birth. The debt we owe to the play of imagination is incalculable.

—Carl Gustav Jung

Coming up...

In the next chapter we look at some simple ways of guiding your thinking into higher, more effective states of mind.

7

TRACKING THE SIGNS OF HIGH-PERFORMANCE THINKING
Built-in Compass

The way you use Thought determines whether you can lead a meeting at high-quality, productive levels—and draw others toward higher states of mind. The higher the quality of participants' thinking, the more successful and enjoyable the meeting will be. There are some simple ways to know you are on the right track to high performance states of mind.

Tracking is the art of being able to follow the trail of an animal or person in the wild. If you followed a skilled tracker in the wild, you might think he had some magical power to divine the path of the animal he was tracking. No matter how much you looked, you would see nothing to mark the path. If the tracker taught you about the spoor and signs, however, you would, with practice, develop a proficient eye for tracking. The signs were always there; they simply meant nothing to your uneducated eye. The tracker must have clear vision to follow the trail; he cannot wear blinders and expect to be successful.

Tracking human interactions

Tracking matters of the heart—relationships, teamwork, synergy, and creativity—is no different. In order to work with people effectively at home, at work, and in meetings, we, like the tracker, must develop eyes to recognize Thought in its many forms. Fortunately, it turns out that each of us is born with a natural, healthy way of using the power of Thought, which brings us eyes for the obvious. If we have our bearings, we naturally notice elements about people that are helpful in bringing out the best in them. Their moods, receptivity, mental barriers, mindsets, and innate motivations are obvious. We see the effect of our own mental state on them, and how they are reacting to what we say. Reflective listening (which we discussed in Chapter 2) takes us to a deeper level of rapport and leaves people feeling truly understood and respected. None of this requires effort or special talent. It is an inherent ability that is invaluable in guiding highly effective meetings. Once the role of Thought begins to become obvious and instinctive, you will find it pretty easy to guide people toward higher, healthier states of mind.

Being centered

This creative, healthy way of using Thought is the most natural thing in the world. In fact, it is something you have already experienced in your daily life. However, without the trained eyes of the tracker, you might not have recognized it as such. Here are just a few examples of signs that you are in a healthy use of Thought.

You are using Thought in your natural, healthy manner when you...

...feel alive and wonderful for no reason at all

...have a realization or insight

...get hit with a blinding flash of the obvious and see a brilliant solution to a vexing challenge

...feel in a vacation state of mind

...are totally involved in your favorite hobby like gardening, golfing, hiking, or fishing

...find yourself completely relaxed in the shower or bath

...are inspired in a brainstorming session

...are alert, clear, and present in an emergency

...are quiet and reflective

...see the natural humor in life

...feel compassion and understanding toward someone

...are "on your game" in a sport or your occupation

I'm pointing out how available this healthy use of Thought is, because this is where you want to be in leading or influencing any meeting. The higher your state of mind, the more influence you have in drawing others to their own health. People in higher states of mind tend to more readily see to the heart of issues and find solutions or make sound decisions.

When we lose contact with our healthy use of Thought, we notice some very different feelings and experiences. (Remember, your innate, healthy use of Thought is always there, but sometimes you override it with not-so-healthy thinking.) You can be sure you have lost touch with your healthy use of Thought when you...

...over-think, ruminate, or worry

...feel stressed, pressured, burdened, or serious

...analyze habitually

...listen critically so that people feel patronized and cut off

...are distracted or revved up

...are busy-minded (juggling several things in your active thinking at the same time)

...are angry, irritated, bored, sad, or depressed

...are blaming others

...are in that "get it done at any cost" mode

...are not having fun

...find life devoid of humor

This is not where you want to be to run an effective meeting.

Lost? No problem

Losing your bearings (moving out of a healthy use of Thought) is quite natural from time to time. A Chief Financial Officer (CFO) might handle numbers effortlessly in healthy thinking. In the next moment, while feeling inadequate dealing with people, he might lose his bearings and come across as cold and uncaring. An Art Director might come up with brilliant concepts and bring out the best in her staff when she is operating in her natural, healthy use of Thought. Sitting down to work on next year's budget, however, she might find herself losing her bearings—grinding away in stress.

When we are in the natural, healthy use of Thought, we can handle any task in our day effectively and effortlessly. It is only insecure thinking and habits that trick us away from our natural ability. Deeper understanding about the principles of Mind, Consciousness, and Thought will eventually guide us, as well as the CFO and Art Director, back to our high state of mental functioning, regardless of the task.

Keys to staying on track

Gaining a firmer footing for staying in the healthy use of Thought requires getting the "feel" of it and resolving to spend as much time there as you can each day. The second key is to recognize that everybody loses his or her bearings from time to time. It is easy to recognize when you lose your bearings by noticing how you feel. If you are experiencing pressure, stress, negative emotions, or discouragement, or if you are behaving in a harsh manner, then you have lost your bearings. The trick is to recognize when you are lost and

KNOW that if you relax and quiet down you will naturally return to your health.

Like the tracker on the trail, you develop an instinctive sense for staying on the path of health. You learn how it feels when your thinking gets off track; you feel your spirits lower and you sense that things have become more difficult. You also know how it feels when you are cruising in your natural, healthy use of Thought. You feel hopeful and creative, you have a high learning curve, you know instinctively how to bring out the best in people, and you produce your best work. With this feeling compass, you simply enjoy and feel grateful in health and take the times when you are lost with a philosophical grain of salt. Your tolerance for being away from your health goes down, and you naturally spend more and more time in your healthy use of Thought.

Recognizing the quality of your thinking and its direct link to your moment-to-moment experience is quite simple once you have the feel for it. Even the most lost person in the world has times when his mind clears and he bounces back to healthy thinking. It might only be in the shower or during an emergency, but it happens. Similarly, the most creative, well-adjusted person still has times when she loses her bearings and derails. The actual time each day you spend in health is not the point. What matters is that you realize that health is your natural state—and trust that you will spend more and more time in health as your understanding deepens.

Summing up

Since your feelings and emotions, both positive and negative, reflect your thinking moment to moment, they serve as a valuable compass to guide you along the track of healthy functioning. When you recognize that you have lost your bearings, you simply need to stop, clear your head, relax, and let your healthy use of Thought dominate again.

Operating more of the time in natural healthy use of Thought gives you leverage in meetings. Your healthy, light, wiser state of mind will tend to draw the meeting tone to higher levels. This wiser perspective will also help you to see to the heart of issues more quickly where others may get bogged down. This in itself helps produce more results in less time—and makes it possible for people to enjoy a meeting. As they sense your healthy state of mind, other people will be drawn to operate more from their own healthy use of Thought.

Our life is shaped by our mind; we become what we think.

—Ancient Buddhist scripture

Coming up...

Getting a "feel" for when a meeting is on or off track.... Chapter 8 explores the critical variable that determines just how successful a meeting can be.

8

WHAT MAKES A GOOD MEETING?
Tangible Intangibles

A successful meeting is one in which participants accomplish the purpose of the meeting and feel uplifted and better connected. Successful meetings don't just happen; they result from skillful design, an understanding of the human factor, and a bit of luck. You can learn skillful design and tap into the commonsense understanding of the human factor. And that's how you set the stage for luck.

I have asked many managers what makes a bad meeting. The most common response is that a bad meeting is one in which nothing is accomplished. Yet on further probing, most managers can recall great meetings in which nothing tangible was accomplished. That is, no decisions were made and no information was communicated. They can also recall meetings in which there were many tangible results, yet people did not leave the meeting feeling good about it.

Do you send people away from a meeting feeling that it was worthwhile, regardless of tangible results? What does the meeting manager need to know in order to run a successful meeting?

Tangible intangibles

The answer is fairly straightforward. It rests in understanding the power of Thought in creating personal experience. There is a tangible and intangible element to a good meeting—an objective and a subjective dimension. You can run a meeting where you cover all of the agenda and make the necessary decisions but leave people feeling abused or worn out. You can also have a nice, warm, fuzzy meeting and accomplish none of the objectives. To put both together requires an understanding of the dynamics of meetings and the nature of people, as well as good planning.

Tone: the bellwether of meeting quality

Your most reliable guide throughout a meeting is the tone or feeling of the meeting. The tone of a meeting is *everything.* As we mentioned in an earlier chapter, the tone of a meeting is the compilation of individual states of mind. Figure 8-1 shows an arbitrary range of meeting tones and corresponding quality levels of thinking that you might encounter. The higher and lighter the meeting tone, the more creative and proactive participants are and the better they feel about the meeting. A low-tone meeting, regardless of how much is accomplished, can leave people worn out and feeling it was a waste of time—or at least not worth the effort.

MEETING TONE

Meeting Tone	Quality of Individual Thinking
Exhilarating	Brilliant
Inspiring	Insightful
Uplifting	Creative
Enjoyable	Collaborative
Neutral	Cooperative
Tense	Defensive
Stressed	Argumentative
Adversarial	Reactive
Bogged down	Dull
Discouraging	Grinding

Figure 8-1

No doubt everyone would have their own idea of a scale, but the notion here is that meetings do operate at different tone levels. In fact, during even the best meetings, things may get sluggish as well as uplifting. As a general rule, if you charted the tone of a typical meeting it might look something like Figure 8-2.

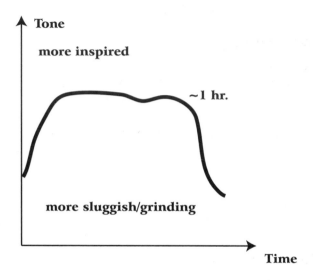

Figure 8-2

The tone invariably drops after about an hour in most meetings, because people begin to think too analytically, get tired, become preoccupied with their own agenda, or grow distracted by thoughts about what else they should be doing. In other words, people's personal thinking drops the tone.

If you pay attention to the tone of any meeting, you will notice that it indeed goes up and down. At the beginning, when things need to start cooking, the tone usually rises. After a while, the tone will drop. When the tone takes a serious drop—whether from fatigue, too much detail, or conflict—it is time to intervene. Many of our clients appoint a tone monitor for the meeting whose job it is to pay attention to tone and bring declining tone to the group's attention. The knowledgeable meeting leader has a number of tools at his or her disposal to guide the meeting tone. We'll discuss these tools in some depth in Chapter 17.

Summing up

Tone is everything. Like a race car mechanic who listens to the engine to know whether it is tuned for optimum performance, the savvy leader pays attention to a meeting's tone. The higher and lighter the tone, the more creative, wise, and proactive the thinking. This higher tone produces better results and leaves people feeling renewed rather than worn out.

The actuality of life is thought.

—**Aristotle**

Coming up...

Ready for relationships? Next up is a commonsense primer on relationships that will offer you insight into how to bring out the best in individuals and teams.

DYNAMICS

9

PERSON TO PERSON
Relationship Essentials

The ability to deal effectively with people and foster healthy relationships is essential to running high-impact meetings. The good news is that healthy relationships—and their attendant feelings of respect, rapport, openness, and ease— come naturally when we operate in our innate, healthy use of Thought. It is only when our memories, habits, and personal thinking get in the way that we have relationship difficulties.

Entire books exist on the subject of interpersonal relationships, and it may seem pretentious to attempt to cover the subject in a few words. But by focusing on the key driver—Thought—we can get to the essentials directly.

In my work with organizational teams and interpersonal relationships of all types, I have realized a few key points that will help anyone find greater ease in relationships. Skill-ful handling of relationships is a definite asset in running high-functioning meetings, because it helps you create a climate for high-performance states of mind.

Listening

One critical piece of understanding is **reflective listening**. This means hearing the speaker with no personal thought interference *so that he or she feels understood*. I covered this important topic in depth in Chapter 2. You will recall that unconditional respect and listening without agenda or judgment are the keys.

Inner guidance

Intuitive navigation is the second piece. In the normal course of working with people, the relationship dynamic between individuals is constantly in flux. It is just not possi-ble to figure out intellectually what is going on with someone else. For example, you might be presenting an idea in a meeting when suddenly one of the key participants reacts and draws back from the discussion. There is no way for you to know what he reacted to, nor is it necessarily appropriate to pursue it. These moments are what we might call major intersections. You can head in any one of several directions, and you don't know which is most appropriate. In this example, you might ignore his reaction and barrel on, you might stop and ask for comments or objections, or you might take a break.

Since *you cannot figure out* the right choice in the moment, you have to rely on something else—your instinctive naviga-tion. It's simple: If you are not consumed with your own per-sonal thinking but remain relaxed in your healthy use of Thought, you will have a feeling or sense about the moment—like a blip on the radar screen. If you choose an inappropriate direction, your feeling will grow worse. You will feel a tightness, tension, and negativity that indicates what you are doing is not working. If you choose a direction that makes things easier, you'll feel the tension relax and the people will be drawn back into the group.

Like a ship at sea, the navigation equipment is always indicating location and course, but the helmsman may not always pay attention to it. I can't tell you how many times I've had the gnawing feeling that what I'm saying or doing at the moment isn't right. Instead of respecting my intuition and stepping back to find the humility to stop, I have allowed my intellect or ego to override my gut feeling and have drifted into deeper problems. Later I'll kick myself and say, "Why didn't I pay attention to what I felt at the time?" With practice, we learn to trust our instinctive navigation. I find it essential in dealing with anyone to pay attention to that resource. I know a lot of business people shun the so-called "soft side." I also know that most of them do respect their intuition and rely on it when making decisions.

Forgiveness: the magic eraser

The other essential element in successful relationships is *forgiveness*. Hanging onto resentment, anger, and ill will is a total waste of time—and it prevents us from enjoying our natural health. Forgiveness is like a magic slate—it gives us a fresh start. Without forgiveness, we hold grudges and harbor bad feelings. These negative thoughts and resulting feelings contaminate meetings. Instead of being synergistic and open to new ideas, those of us who bear resentment remain negative and closed. This baggage will poison a meeting.

When I talk with clients about forgiveness, I find that many people have some fairly strong ideas about the subject. Among the more common is that if you forgive someone who harmed you, they will feel it is okay to do it again. Somehow they see forgiveness as akin to condoning. Another is that those people need to be punished with your ill will—they deserve it. Still another is that forgiveness is letting people off the hook. I suppose there are plenty more reasons people use to justify not forgiving. But none of them stands up in the light of healthy common sense.

Simple logic

Let's look at forgiveness from a logical standpoint. Feeling resentment and ill will toward someone who has lied, sandbagged, or politically outmaneuvered you is certainly common—and you may feel totally justified in bearing the ill will. Nevertheless, it's just not helpful to you. Which brings me to the main point of this discussion: Forgiveness is not for the perpetrator—**it's for you**. In fact, you need never let the other person know that you have forgiven him or her.

Forgiving is letting go completely without condoning. If you can forgive and forget whatever happened, you are free of that burden in your thinking. Otherwise, that ill feeling acts like a lead weight on the spirit. Every time you see him or hear his name you are visited by those bad feelings again. So forgiveness is quite selfish—and very practical.

Accountability: paying the price

What about accountability for the perpetrator's actions? Forgiveness and accountability are two different issues. Oprah Winfrey did a show once on people who had lost family members to drunk drivers. On stage were six or eight mothers and fathers, husbands and wives who had lost a loved one due to the recklessness of a drunken driver. Generally, they were irate and angry about their losses, and quite hostile toward drunken drivers. Some of the incidents had occurred years before, but they were still angry as they talked (Thought) about it.

In the audience was a mother whose daughter had been killed a month before by a drunk driver. Unlike the people on the stage, she was not angry; she seemed serene and centered. Oprah asked about that, and the mother said she had forgiven the man who killed her son. The audience was stunned.

Oprah asked, "How could you forgive this man?"

"I did it for myself," the woman replied. "My anger and bad feelings toward him were eating me alive. It is bad enough to have lost my daughter. I just could not bear more bad feelings."

"Does that mean you don't think he should have to pay for his crime?" Oprah challenged.

"Absolutely not," the woman assured her. "He is awaiting trial and must pay the price for what he did. I had to let it go—to forgive him—for my peace of mind, to help me heal."

You probably won't run into something quite that intense in a meeting, but this example shows the wisdom and power of forgiveness. In this chapter, I will spend a lot of time on forgiveness because I encounter so much ill will in meetings.

What it takes to forgive

So how do you go about finding forgiveness when you are riddled with resentment?

Finding forgiveness requires three things:

1) **The desire to forgive.** You want to stop harboring the bad feelings for *your* sake.

2) **A feeling of compassion toward the perpetrator**—whether or not he or she deserves it.

3) **A willingness to let it go.** It's over and you move on without the baggage.

Don't mistake what I'm saying as excusing his or her actions. People must be held accountable. When the law covers the action that has triggered your ill will, then it is up to the law to handle the consequences. That is no guarantee that they won't get off, of course. Regardless, the consequences are not your business. The more challenging situation is the person in your life (even a friend) who has somehow "done you wrong" in your eyes. Depending on the severity of the transgression, the consequence may be a lost friendship or just a case of deep disappointment in your friend's behavior. Consequences are not necessarily punishment. Even a jail term for a drunk driver convicted of manslaughter may not seem like appropriate punishment for a life needlessly lost. For example, if you misjudge your available room in passing another car, the consequence may be a wreck. Similarly, if you slander someone you may face a lawsuit.

As tempting as it is, you simply cannot afford to indulge debilitating thinking about making sure the perpetrator pays the price. Revenge extracts a heavy price from your equanimity and health. It helps if you realize that whoever wronged you either does not realize what she had done, or lives in a troubled state of mind that you can feel grateful not to inhabit.

Let's go through these three requisites to forgiveness one at a time. The desire to forgive has to come from your common sense. It will mean getting beyond whatever beliefs you've accumulated about the value of maintaining ill feelings (punishment, prevention). People can tell you it's a good idea to forgive and forget, but only you can decide to head in that direction. Again, this is for **your** well-being. I had a client years ago who was unwilling to forgive and let go of the resentment he held for his wife. His ill feelings provided the perfect excuse for him to avoid making a decision about his marriage. If he forgave her, then he would have to make a decision to recommit himself to the marriage or to end it. As long as he felt the ill will, he was immobilized in his decision making about a marriage that had lost its luster.

Finding compassion for someone who has wronged, harmed, or disappointed you is sometimes difficult. **Finding the compassion to forgive requires that you simultaneously see the offender's pain *and* psychological innocence.** Recognizing the unhappy, unhealthy world of a person who commits unconscionable acts has helped me most. For example, let's take a look at the manager who is always difficult to deal with and habitually maneuvers for power in the organization. This manager may run down colleagues, hoard information, and play politics with fervor. Imagine living in a world so stressful, pressured, and unhappy that you see fellow managers as threats—competitors to be vanquished.

Let's go back to an earlier principle about Thought and experience that we talked about in Chapter 5 (the Thought-Reality Cycle) and look at this manager.

Thought ➤ Feeling ➤ State of Mind ➤ Behavior ➤ Result ➤ Thought

Whatever action someone takes (including this manager) makes sense to him at the time. Every behavior starts with a thought, and that thought represents certain logic to the thinker. When the manager is in his natural, healthy use of Thought (feeling secure and good about himself, perhaps even inspired), then the resultant state of mind and logic (thinking) is high quality. The resulting behavior will more than likely work out well for all involved. If the manager begins to feel insecure (entertaining insecure thoughts and doubts), then his state of mind drops. As a result, only lower quality thinking (habits, memories) is available, which leads to actions that don't work out well. Nevertheless, he is doing the best he can—given his state of mind and the quality of thought available to him at that moment. In that sense, **all of us are truly *psychologically* innocent.** We just didn't know any better at the time. Our EQ (emotional intelligence) dropped to single digits and we did stupid things.

Does this explanation excuse his behavior? Absolutely not! It just gives us the understanding to stop harboring ill feelings. Our bad feelings toward him rarely reform his behavior. If nothing else, feel grateful that you don't have to live inside his head.

Let's look at the person who drinks in excess. He is feeling stressed, pressured, perhaps even tormented by his thinking. He finds that a few drinks blot out the bad feeling. Perhaps a few more deaden him enough that he actually feels relaxed. This cycle is self-reinforcing, so it tends to continue. The fact that he does not have sense enough not to drive is equally clear. Anyone who has ever had a few drinks knows that you don't think as wisely and clearly as when you are sober. Combine this impaired judgment with lengthened reaction times, and you have a recipe for disaster. The point is that given the troubled state of his mind when sober and his desire to deaden the pain and feel better, he took a remedial course that made sense to him at the time. Understanding this helps us drop our ill feelings and return to our state of health. Nevertheless, the drunk driver must still be held accountable for his actions.

Here is a humbling personal experience about compassion that illustrates how easily our own thinking can trap us. A colleague (we'll call her Ann) came to me with problems in her marriage. She was a beginning teacher of the principle-based understanding on which this book is based. As I worked with her, she finally confided that she had been hooked on crack cocaine for years. Of course, I was stunned. When I finally regained my composure, I spent several days helping her find her innate resource of healthy thinking and feelings of natural well-being. When she left, she confided that she had never felt so well, so relaxed and at peace. She swore that she was finished with drugs.

Two weeks later, her husband called and said that she was back into it. I instantly became upset. How could she do that, I thought. *She knows better.* I felt let down, and every time I thought of her I felt judgment and disappointment. I certainly was not finding compassion or seeing any innocence.

When she called again for help, I could not work with her because she instantly detected my judgment. A week later, her husband called and said she was in the emergency room with a heart attack caused by the drug.

At that instant, it hit me. This poor soul was truly lost from her natural health. She did not know any better and was in big trouble. I immediately felt all judgment and ill will vanish, and I felt nothing but compassion and love for her. I'm happy to say that Ann eventually rose above the habit and is now living in good health—free from drugs. My thoughts (judgments and expectations) had prevented me from finding compassion and forgiveness. I could not see her psychological innocence because of my thinking that of all people, *she* should know better.

How does all of this apply to meetings?

We have been pointing to the value of conducting high-tone meetings. Since the meeting tone is a result of the collective states of mind of the participants, it is important to be able to bring out the best in each person. Optimizing your relationships with each person in that room helps everyone to relax into his or her natural, healthy use of Thought. If you harbor ill will, bad memories, or negative attitudes toward even one person in the room, it will tend to dampen the spirit of the meeting. If several people are doing the same thing, it will be challenging to get the meeting off the ground.

If you are running the meeting, something as simple as personally greeting each person as he or she arrives and exchanging a few words to reconnect can be a good start. I know leaders who start their meetings by going around the room asking each participant to briefly share his or her latest "win" or positive experience. The idea is to help people clear the air and get in the moment.

Summing up

When you put all this information together in the context of meetings, it looks like this: You want to have your relationships with and between the attendees as healthy as possible. Paying attention to your feeling compass and your intuition keeps you headed in a constructive direction. When you feel that things have gotten off track, stop and listen. If people say or do things that hurt your feelings, don't take it personally. Recognize that they are off balance, that the quality of their thinking is low, and that they are therefore doing the best they can. If you do "lose it," get over it and let it go (forgive others and yourself) as quickly as possible so that you can return to a healthy, wise state. That way, you'll be able to participate more effectively and contribute and learn more in meetings.

Remember, whatever your experience, it always, always starts with a thought.

The intuitive mind is a sacred gift and the rational mind is a faithful servant. We have created a society that honors the servant and has forgotten the gift.

—**Albert Einstein**

Coming up...

Look out, conflict in the meeting. Next on the docket is a look at an effective approach to evolving conflict into a meeting of the minds.

NOTES AND REMINDERS

Worry is like a rocking chair—it gives you something to do but it doesn't get you anywhere.
—**Dorothy Galyean**

10

CONFLICT EVOLUTION
A Meeting of the Minds

Conflict in a meeting becomes a problem only when it drags down the tone. Skillful guidance of the tone can turn disruptive conflict into stimulating discussion and consensus building. Getting consensus does not mean that everyone is in agreement—only that they can live with it.

The difference between hostile conflict and constructive disagreement/debate is in the tone or thinking quality; in other words, the intensity and amount of ill will. As we discussed earlier in Chapter 4, everyone constructs his or her unique private world of beliefs, values, opinions, and thoughts. When challenged, the intensity with which people defend their worldview depends on how much they value the issue and how well they understand the role of Thought in creating their personal world. People who identify closely with their personal world most often have a strong view of what is right and wrong. People who see their personal thinking with some perspective more often tend to be open to understanding another person's thinking and worldview. In any case, conflict is something you will encounter some time or another in a meeting.

When conflict is an asset

Healthy differences in viewpoint can often help to deepen everyone's understanding of an issue. But whether the meeting becomes polarized and stymied in heated emotions, or whether it moves toward a wiser perspective for everyone, depends in great part on how the meeting leader handles conflict. In general, the object of handling conflict is to transform it into a constructive force.

Perhaps the single most important element in evolving conflict to a wiser level is REFLECTIVE LISTENING, as discussed in Chapter 2. The importance of listening in transforming conflict is this: **People tend to not listen until they *feel* listened to and understood. In order to understand people, we must be willing to listen respectfully, without a position.** This is what Stephen Covey, in his *Seven Habits of Successful Leaders*, means when he advises leaders to "…understand before you seek to be understood."

Listen, listen, listen

As soon as it becomes obvious from the tone of the meeting that the discussion has changed to open conflict accompanied by ill feeling, the meeting leader needs to intervene. The people doing the arguing are seldom the ones doing the listening. In fact, others in the meeting will often notice that no one is listening—everybody's talking instead. At this point, listening becomes your main job.

Not only do you need to listen as a meeting leader, you also need to step in and guide the listening of the group. (You can do this, of course, even if you are not leading the meeting. It is just easier when you are running the show.) The simplest way is for you to start asking questions of one of the parties and LISTENING to his or her responses. You will need a firm hand in averting the tendency of other parties to jump in and argue. Usually you need only say something like "We'll get to your side of this in a few minutes, but first I want to understand in depth what he is saying here." You pursue deep listening until the speaker feels understood. Remember, people are not as inclined to continue to push their opinions once they feel they have really been understood. Once that is handled, you go to the other side of the conflict and do the same thing. This process may require several iterations, but by the time you complete it everyone in the meeting will have probed both sides and their own reactions.

This kind of listening—what I call impartial, non-judgmental inquiry—makes it possible for people to see something about their own thinking and positions. The deeper you listen, the more obvious the speaker's thinking will become to everyone: his assumptions, his definition and perception of the problem, his predispositions, possible blind spots about possible solutions, impact on other departments, and so on. Through this skillful listening, you are helping the group better understand the speaker's position, and you are helping the speaker see his or her own thinking about the issue more clearly. As this happens with each side, the group begins to connect with common threads that may lead to a wiser solution than anyone had seen before. Done well, this powerful listening can ignite a new level of synergy in the group. Without it, the meeting is likely to become mired in and focused on differences. These differences can come to seem irreconcilable.

Consensus

If you are getting input from participants at a meeting but will make the decision on your own, then you probably have everything you need. You can thank everyone and close the meeting. More often, however, it is important to get a buy-in or meeting of the minds among those present. If so, then you need to take another step. Remember, *consensus is not about getting everyone to agree.* Consensus is about getting to the point where every person feels listened to and understood—*and can live with the final decision*. The key to getting a meeting of the minds is to move people toward mutual appreciation and respect. It is in this spirit that they can begin to build on areas of agreement, rather than remain mired in areas of discord.

Working from agreement—critical parameters

One direction that seems to help in guiding people toward a meeting of the minds is to list the areas of agreement that became obvious to you as you listened. As you list each one, get concurrence from everyone that this is indeed an area of agreement. If even one person does not agree, then you need to listen more. As you list these areas, people in the meeting will nearly always begin to see that they are in accord on some major issues and just need to work out some minor differences. The spirit of cooperation and mutual respect will propel this discussion toward a meeting of the minds.

For example, suppose that you are chairing a meeting of the office support staff and the topic of discussion is the purchase of a new document center. Imagine that prior to the meeting, you assigned three people to look into three different brands of machine, one brand per person. In the meeting, let's imagine that opinionated groups form around each of the three possibilities. No resolution seems possible, because each time one group champions a feature of their preferred machine, another opinionated group claims that theirs is better.

Here's how you could approach the situation: Ask everyone in the meeting exactly what the machine the company purchases must be able to do, and list these parameters. Verify that everyone agrees on each performance criterion. In our example, imagine that after some reflection the following list of parameters emerges that the entire group agrees on point by point: The machine must be able to:

- duplicate any size from 5 x 8 to 11 x 14

- print at minimum rate of 25 pages/minute

- enlarge and reduce by a factor of 200%

- produce color prints as well as crisp black and white

The machine must also:

- be simple for the support staff to operate and supply

- have a vendor who can service it within 2 hours of a call

- cost no more than $X to purchase or less than $Y/month to lease

You then get agreement that any machine that meets these criteria is acceptable to the group. Once everyone is in agreement on this point, then the choice is usually clear, simple, and sometimes arbitrary.

With some complex issues you still may have some areas of disagreement at this point in your meeting. You can approach any remaining areas of disagreement in the spirit of creative cooperation. "How can we resolve this so that all parties feel good about it?" When it is over, there may be one or two items that will fall into the category of "agree to disagree"—that is, reasonable minds could disagree, but virtually no ill will remains.

No hard feelings

If every conflict is transformed into a meeting of the minds or an agreement to disagree, then there are no hard feelings. This type of closure to an issue allows people to remain free to devote their energies to matters at hand rather than fuming about losing out. Agreeing to disagree simply means that we do not see a wiser level where we might agree, and reasonable minds might certainly disagree about this issue. No one is right and no one is wrong. Emotionally, we let go of our position, understanding that the discussion did not result in swaying the other person to our position. Each side felt strongly enough about the soundness of their position—even after open listening—that they were not willing to let it go. That's life. But everyone on both sides of the dispute at least sees that the other position is viable. *Remember, it is crucial that everyone be able to walk away willing to live with the decision.*

The key is for people to be able to walk away clean. You want them in at least a neutral state. If some action must be taken one way or the other, then the person in charge must make an arbitrary call. However, if there is even one person in the group who truly cannot live with the decision, then it seems to me that you have to listen more. There is something that you and the rest of the group does not understand to that person's satisfaction. Once that person feels truly understood, he or she will be able to live with whatever decision is made. Remember that people want to be heard and understood, even if you don't agree with them.

In one of the school board meetings I chaired, a group of upset parents descended on the board like a swarm of angry bees. When we opened the meeting to public comment, they began an emotional attack on the school's special education programs, the teachers, and the board. They did not feel that the special education children were receiving proper attention. The teachers immediately rallied to defend the program, explaining that scarce funds limited the services. After a few minutes, I gently cut off the emerging debate and began deep listening so that we could all understand these upset parents. When a teacher or another board member tried to defend our position, I was steadfast in insisting we just listen.

After 20 minutes of parents venting their dissatisfaction, they began to quiet down. We summarized the substance of what we understood to be their major complaints. At this point, I stated that one thing seemed apparent from all comments: there was a problem with the special education program. Everyone agreed that what I said was true (though, of course, few could agree on what or who was responsible).

Next, I asked the staff whether the problems as presented were something within the school's power to solve. The answer was no, and the parents agreed. We then determined that it was the County Office of Education who had the responsibility and the authority to actually remedy the problem. Everyone agreed. The board then committed to arranging a special meeting with the Deputy Superintendent of Education who was in charge of special education programs. Even though we were not able to reach a solution during the meeting, as a group we were able to convert the emotional conflict into positive action leading to a sensible solution. The upset parents left the meeting feeling they had been heard and that we were taking action. We all had come to a meeting of the minds in defining the problem and laying out the appropriate action. No one left the meeting feeling upset about this issue.

It's seldom personal

Many of us have trouble with conflict because it usually appears to be a personal attack, especially when someone is challenging our deeply held views. It takes some perspective to understand that what is going on is simply people express-ing their own views. The more caught up people get in their personal views, the more emotional they become, the less they listen, and the more they talk. Some people may be closely attached to their thinking (views); others may realize that what they think is not "how it is" but just their thinking at the moment. If you are the one "under attack," step back and don't take it personally. It's not worth losing your bear-ings.

The key to handling this kind of heated conflict in a meeting is to ensure that everyone feels respectfully under-stood and truly heard. As the meeting, leader it is your job to take charge and do something about it. Your respectful, reflective listening will guide others. Remember, you can always take a break, lighten things up with some humor, listen, move on to something else, or reschedule the topic for another time. Indulging caustic attacks and disrespect is a certain recipe for lingering problems later on.

Summing up

By paying attention to the tone, it is possible to turn con-flict into a stimulating discussion. When things get heated, it is time to do a lot of listening. Through reflective listening, areas of agreement and alignment will become obvious. Building on these areas of agreement is the foundation for evolving the conflict so that the group reaches a meeting of the minds or agrees to disagree. Either position works, because it does not leave people with resentful feelings and the need to drag their feet or sabotage decisions.

Conditions for creativity are to be puzzled; to concentrate; to accept conflict and tension; to be born everyday; to feel a sense of self.
—**Erich Fromm**

Coming up...

Next, in Chapter 11, I show you how to set up decision making in a meeting so that you achieve good decisions with a minimum of aggravation and wasted time. I will talk about how to make sure you get maximum buy-in for the decisions.

11

DECISION–INDECISION
Teeter-Totter of Turmoil

In a meeting, over-analysis and fear can put people on the horns of a dilemma without a resolution in sight. At some point, clarity must reign and someone has to make a decision. However, it's important to be forthright and clear from the beginning about who that someone is. Such clarity leads to better decisions, less backlash, and better meeting tone that supports wiser decision-making.

In this chapter, I will discuss two keys to achieving wise decision-making in meetings: a clear mind and clear communication about who will be making the final decision.

Clearing the mind

In personal, individual decision-making, a clear head, unburdened by worry or a busy mind crowded with thoughts vying for attention, is the best resource for wise decisions. First, you must quiet down into your natural, healthy use of Thought. Second, reflect on the situation and whatever input you have, then allow the wisest decision to emerge. If you don't see a wise choice at the moment, put it on the back burner (as described in Chapter 6) and allow your creative resources to work in the background.

At some point, an answer or idea will strike you, or you just have to call it like you see it. That's the best you can do. Sometimes an answer hits you in the shower, on the golf course, or on time off when you are not thinking about it. The common factor in all of these scenarios is a clear head. In meetings, the group equivalent of personally clearing your head is to keep the meeting tone light. A light, even inspirational meeting tone helps to keep people from getting bogged down in too much analysis or opinion. This higher, lighter tone tends to bring out wiser, more creative solutions and decisions.

Clearing the air

Ever go to a meeting where the boss asked for your opinion on an issue—and you were quite certain he had already made up his mind before he asked? It's an insult, isn't it? So if you want to upset everyone, leave them feeling patronized, and waste their time, that's a good approach. But if you want to run meetings at a high level, make them count, and have people feel that their time and input is valued, then it is important to tell the group up front what you expect. As long as the group understands the nature of the decision process, there will be few hard feelings.

Here are the most common types of decisions in meetings and suggestions for how to handle them wisely.

Decision Type #1: DONE DEAL

This situation usually involves the CEO or a senior executive. In this case, the executive has already made the decision and simply wants to handle any questions or resistance. When you are the leader in this situation, you want to state clearly that the decision is not open to question—it has already been made. You are open to discussing the logic and rationale, implications, questions, and applications.

This type of decision-making is the least popular, because people feel they are being dictated to. The price you pay in this case is a diminished buy-in from those affected.

Here are two examples when you might find the done deal appropriate:

- a decision you had to make because of a time urgency
- a decision only you can make, such as budget cutbacks, downsizing, new direction for the company, or acquisitions
- a mandate or edict handed down from your boss or the Board of Directors

Decision Type #2: MY DECISION. I have a bias but am open to input

These are decisions that you are not willing to delegate, but you wisely want input from the group before deciding. You must genuinely be open to changing your thinking or this process will backfire. People can sense when you are predisposed, so it is helpful to be honest from the start and tell them how you see it. If you don't, you will generate ill will, lower the tone of the meeting, and send people away in various states of upset and resentment. All of that diminishes the effectiveness of people. You might say something like, "I am going to make a decision about XYZ, but I want to hear your input before I do." If you are leaning one way or another, tell them, "I'm leaning in favor of XYZ, but I have not made up my mind." Or you might say, "Unless I am persuaded differently, I plan to take this action."

A hidden agenda is deadly in a meeting. When you have something on your mind that you are not communicating openly, people react by feeling irritated. Not knowing what it is about, they will likely make up something. Success in this situation depends on listening with an open mind. (See Chapter 2.)

Decision Type #3: GROUP DECISION. I want to reach consensus on this

This type of decision is one of the more common challenges for a staff. The boss wisely realizes that making a decision that everyone can support will go a long way toward achieving alignment and getting it implemented quickly. These decisions include obvious things such as:

- pursuing a new market
- developing a new product
- offering a new service
- adding a new product line
- embarking on a company-wide strategy like total quality management, or re-engineering (where a fresh look at the organizational structure usually leads to a streamlined, more efficient organization), or just-in-time purchasing
- development of a new corporate culture.

The key to success is managing the tone of the meeting and ensuring that contributors feel <u>listened to and understood</u>. Focusing on what you do agree on rather than what you don't keeps the spirit of the meeting on track. (See Chapter 8.)

Decision Type #4: YOUR DECISION. I will support whatever you decide

These are generally not top-level decisions, but items that have no strategic consequence or that fall within the purview of a subordinate. Some examples might include:

- decisions about equipment and personnel within budget constraints
- location for the company picnic
- specifics for redecorating the employee lunch room
- choosing the employee of the month
- travel to customers (although more companies are requiring top-level approval)

In this case, the executive in charge must leave the final decision up to the group if it is within the initial parameters established. For example, the executive might tell the group the maximum budget allowed for the company picnic and that the location should not be more than a half-hour drive from the company headquarters. Whatever the group decides, the executive must stand behind it. Overruling the group decision would undermine confidence and morale.

Summing up

Sound decisions happen when people have clear information and a clear head. Keeping a sharp eye on the tone of the meeting will move people to wiser levels of decision-making and buy-in. To keep people from dropping into lower states of mind, be clear about the nature of the decision and what role the group has in the decision. Patronizing and evasiveness always backfire. It is not necessary for everyone to agree with a decision. It is only necessary that people reach a point where they can go along with the decision "because reasonable minds could disagree." They may not agree with the decision, but they can live with it.

"Once a decision was made, I did not worry about it afterward."

—**Harry S. Truman**

Coming up...

Caution: opinions ahead. Whenever problems or decisions of any kind surface, you will soon find that people feel obligated to express their opinions on the matter. Sharing opinions can be a great source of insight and stimulation, or it can mire the meeting in quicksand. When the topic degrades into the world of opinion, it is time to intervene. The next chapter will discuss the finer points of how to intervene and guide people toward insight and deeper understanding.

12

OPINIONS
Meeting Catapult or Quagmire

Almost everyone has an opinion on just about everything. How you handle opinions in your meetings determines whether opinions become a stimulator of fresh insight or a closed system of circular thinking. The key is in listening and guiding the tone.

In his classic work *Management: Tasks Responsibilities Practices*, Peter Drucker discusses the vital role of opinions in defining the question to be answered or decision to be made. As Drucker clearly points out, opinions (untested hypotheses) always come first and are essential. Opinions can provide alternatives, healthy disagreement, stimulating exploration, and a challenge to people's thinking and positions. How you handle opinions is an essential element to productive meetings and sound decisions. As always, an understanding of people is essential. It means the difference between opinions that turn a meeting into a quagmire and opinions that act as a springboard to brilliant solutions, decisions, and insight.

When opinions create a quagmire

When meeting participants don't clearly see or know what to do, they usually fall back on their opinions. If an opinion is based on shallow thinking, borrowed positions, or old beliefs, it will most often trigger a flurry of similar low-quality opinions. Opinions usually beget more opinions. You know the meeting has dropped into a quagmire when conflicting opinions pop up like weeds after a spring rain and people are focused on talking and not listening. You will sense the meeting tone drop as you notice these kinds of opinions multiply. The good news is that people seem to be engaged in the issue. To leverage this focus, the meeting leader needs to take the meeting to a deeper level. As before, the key is to guide the group's listening.

If participants are not listening respectfully to each other and you let them go on unguided, nearly everyone will end up stating an opinion—but you may not get much clarity or insight about the issue. Opinions do not necessarily lead to clarity or wise decisions unless the meeting leader handles them well.

When opinions catapult participants into insight, creativity, and solutions

If opinions or positions result from reflection and thoughtful exploration, then they can prove helpful and even essential in identifying the real issue to be decided and in finding viable alternatives. But what happens if the road of opinion does not lead the group in the right direction? What happens if opinions lower the tone? As the meeting leader (or any person willing to intervene), it is time to step in because, left unchecked, indiscriminate opinions can quickly lead to unproductive conflict and hardening of positions. People may not always like your intervention because they love to have free reign with their opinions. Regardless, you will want to guide opinions in the direction that serves the group.

There are two major strategies for directing a meeting locked in opinion to a productive level. These are reflective listening and putting opinions to the test.

Listening

In many if not most meetings I have attended over the years, people seldom listen to understand. Instead, they are thinking about their own opinions, finding fault with what the speaker is saying, or are otherwise distracted and not fully present. Reflective listening to truly understand one another (as described in Chapter 2) is crucial in keeping opinions pointed in a direction that is stimulating and valuable.

Reflective listening serves the meeting in several ways:
- It provides the listener with a good grasp of what the speaker is attempting to communicate.

- The questions that arise out of the desire to truly understand help the speaker clarify his or her own thinking.

- It illuminates the real issue that the speaker is trying to solve. This is especially helpful since the opinion expressed is often not THE issue the meeting needs to be considering. A great answer to the wrong problem or question is not helpful.

The simplest way to get other meeting members to listen more respectfully is to model. If you will simply step in and start the listening process, others are more likely to pick up the direction. Even if they don't, your reflective listening alone may take the discussion to a wiser, more productive level.

Putting opinions to the test

Another important key to the successful handling of opinions is to get people to accept responsibility for their opinions and for the logic that led them to that position. The meeting leader can keep things going in this direction by insisting that the person speaking see his opinion for what it is: a hypothesis. In the world of science, we don't argue about hypotheses; we put them to a test. The same can be true for the world of meetings. The meeting leader would ask the speaker, "What data might validate your hypothesis as a viable approach, solution, or decision?" The speaker might then come up with a simple test or set of data that would prove or disprove her hypothesis (opinion). If other members of the group saw merit in the idea, one or more of them might join her in the process of designing a way to prove or disprove the approach. The speaker might also realize that there seems to be no obvious way to validate her opinion. Overall, this approach will force people to take a deeper look at their own opinions before voicing them. Viewing opinions as hypotheses heads the meeting in a more profound direction.

Both reflective listening and putting opinions to the test help people deepen their thinking and increase their understanding. This type of direction will help the meeting tone stay at healthy and constructive levels—and sometimes it will even reach inspirational heights. When the meeting reaches these higher, healthier levels, it is not unusual for the group to come to solutions and decisions that amaze everyone. It often looks like magic. In fact, it is the natural result of conducting meetings at higher levels.

Last resort

When all else fails, there is one additional, last-resort strategy for redirecting the tone of opinion: Insist that inappropriate opinions stop—that is, if what a person is about to say does not take the group to a wiser level of seeing the issue, then it is not appropriate. This approach is not the most popular type of intervention, especially with those managers who, in the name of fairness, have promoted and supported the habit of eliciting everyone's opinion—despite the fact that the result is often a circular route. So you may have to show people the benefit of turning away from opinion when that route is clearly no longer productive. It is far better for people to sit in the unknown ("I don't see what to do") than to follow the false trail of poorly founded opinion.

By turning away from the known (what is already in your head), you open the door to insight. One insight will take the group beyond the current deadlock and most likely propel the meeting to a higher level where people can leapfrog off each other with fresh ideas and wiser possible solutions. Once the group picks up on this direction, participants will prefer this route of exploring options.

Here is an example. I was attending a public hearing on an issue that was highly controversial in our small community. I don't even recall the issue, but I clearly remember what happened. As soon as the first person gave his opinion on the issue, another jumped up and more adamantly gave hers. Soon people were almost yelling at each other—and the group quickly polarized into at least three factions.

At first, I started evaluating opinions. Each position sounded plausible and persuasive. I quickly found myself confused about which position was the best. At that point I realized I had lost my perspective. I sat back and just listened in a deeper, reflective way—dangling in a state of "not knowing." In a moment of insight, I regained my clarity and raised my hand. "I don't know the best answer. I do know that the sentiment of ill will in this room is so hostile that we as a community will never reach a solution that everyone can live with. We need to be respectful to one another, listen to better understand each position, and look for common ground." This observation spoke to the heart of things, because it stopped the barrage of opinions. Everyone became quiet and reflective, and the next person who talked had a totally different emotional state. This person was respectful and much more humble in suggesting possibilities. The group eventually brought closure to the issue by collectively finding a solution that was wiser than any one person's opinion could have been.

Summing up

Opinions are a welcome sign that people are engaged and care about the outcome. Handled well, opinions are essential to exploring and defining the real issues and discovering viable solutions. Opinions not handled well can drag a meeting down into a morass of thinking that leaves people feeling burnt out and not understood.

Dissent and controversy become meeting stimulants *if* people are respectfully listening to understand one another. Insisting that people treat their opinions as hypotheses and take responsibility for thinking them through and deciding how to prove or disprove them keeps the meeting tone constructive. A little understanding about people and their thinking goes a long way toward transforming a quagmire of opinions into solid meeting results.

"If everybody is thinking alike, then somebody isn't thinking"

—**General George S. Patton**

Coming up...

Open the gates to brainstorming. In Chapter 13 I'll be exploring with you a very special kind of meeting designed specifically for stimulating creative thinking but not geared toward immediate results.

13

BRAINSTORMING
Tapping Original Thought

The main purpose of a brainstorming session is to bring out the endless creativity of every participant in a positive environment of synergy. Done well, a brainstorming session leaves each participant feeling like he or she contributed to every idea.

Getting past what we already know

In most organizations, there comes a time when people want to break the mold, step out of the box of so-called normal thinking, and explore new possibilities. This is the purpose of what have become known as brainstorming sessions. Unlike an ordinary business meeting with structure and agenda, the only purpose of a brainstorming session is to unleash creativity about a particular problem or opportunity. You might find these sessions happening more often in

R&D or artistic departments than in other departments, but sales and marketing will also find such sessions useful from time to time.

Creativity is natural

Everybody is creative. Each of us is born with a resource of original Thought—creativity. Access to innate creativity is as natural as breathing. Many people don't realize this fact and find themselves lost in habits and rituals trying to "be creative." In truth, all we have to do is relax and let our natural access to original Thought flow. You probably know people who you think are exceptionally creative. In comparison, you may feel inadequate in that area. I think you will find that the only real difference is that those creative geniuses have either kept that channel open since childhood or learned to stay out of its way. Staying out of creativity's way just means letting your mind become a conduit for your natural flow of ideas and insights.

Here is an example of a company that depended on creativity for its livelihood but wasn't quite sure how to stay out of creativity's way. My colleague and former partner, George Pransky, worked with a small PR firm that historically held all-nighters when they had trouble coming up with new concepts for their clients' public relations (PR) campaigns. (An example of a PR or advertising concept is the Energizer Bunny). These sessions always started at about 5:00 P.M. Friday afternoon and went on until the wee hours of the next morning. The meeting would start out with lots of ideas that the group picked apart, but eventually the interactions degraded into negativity and discouragement. By 1:00 A.M., everyone was dead tired and out of ideas—asleep on their feet. About that time, everyone would stop judging and trying to figure things out. They would stop talking and just drift. After a while, someone would be struck with a fresh idea. That idea would trigger someone else, and the entire group would gradually come back to life. By 2:00 A.M., they would discover their brilliant new concept.

Because this type of marathon meeting eventually worked despite the ordeal, they had come to believe that it was the only route to creativity. All-nighters had become a habit of the corporate culture. But once these folks developed some understanding about Thought, innate creativity, and meeting tone, they realized they had been wasting a lot of time and energy. With a little diligence and practice, they began to conduct creative sessions that were short, uplifting, and highly effective. They never went back to their all-nighters.

Born out of need

Brainstorming sessions first became popular in the 1960's when business people began to realize they needed a different kind of meeting to foster creativity. These meetings benefited from a skilled facilitator who could keep things positive so that people remained buoyant, hopeful, and upbeat. They also steered participants away from confrontation and judgment, knowing that one idea, however absurd, could trigger insights in the other participants. They also steered participants away from concern about feasibility or practicality. The point was to release as many ideas as possible.

Years ago when I worked in R&D at Arthur D. Little Inc. in Cambridge, Massachusetts, we held informal, brown-bag brainstorming sessions during lunch hour. A Project Manager would invite five or six people to have lunch and kick around a new challenge. The only rule was that no one could invalidate or undermine an idea. The atmosphere was casual but stimulating.

After one such meeting, I asked my boss why he had included a certain person who seemed to be caught up in his air of self-importance and need to dominate the meeting. I wondered why no one had done anything about it. He smiled and said, "Don't worry, he won't be asked to another meeting." He knew that the creative tone of a gathering is very much affected by the state of mind of each participant.

What makes a brainstorming session successful?

We now understand much more clearly why these structured sessions work pretty well. First, they point toward fresh thinking and creativity. Second, they guide people away from the world of opinions, analysis, judgments, and defensiveness. They foster a tone that leads to inspired states of mind.

Conditions that promote innate, creative thinking

As you can see from the prior discussions in Chapters 4 to 7, productive brainstorming sessions demand that people operate in a healthy state of mind. Creativity cannot emerge from memory or analysis, nor does it spring from confrontation or debate. I find that the following tend to promote creativity:

- a safe environment, free of criticism and negativity
- quiet pauses for people to reflect and remain silent from time to time
- encouragement to explore the mystery, the unknown
- support to build on and leapfrog off other people's ideas
- minimal ego and self-interest
- light tone that keeps it fun
- short time span: one hour max!

Tone, tone, tone

Obviously, meeting tone is crucial to a successful brainstorming session. Meeting leaders must stay alert to the tone of the meeting. In fact, it is most helpful to have another person serve as tone monitor. When he or she senses that the tone has dropped (the clues are that people have gotten away from the creative flow into processing, analyzing, and grinding), the tone monitor points it out. You will find that some people are much quicker to pick up on the tone than others. These people will be able to serve well as tone monitors.

Setting the ground rules

If you frequently hold brainstorming meetings, then you will need to do very little in the way of getting off on the right foot. If not, then it works well to gain agreement on a few commonsense meeting guidelines that encompass what I just discussed. Here are some suggested ground rules for successful brainstorming sessions:

- No challenging of another person's ideas.

- If you do not understand someone's idea, then ask respectfully for clarification.

- Rather than point out what you believe is a fallacy in a person's idea, leapfrog by suggesting a new idea that will satisfy that shortcoming. Otherwise, remain silent about it.

- Quiet your thinking and allow fresh ideas to come to you.

- Listen reflectively to let each idea inspire and lead you to insight.

- Beware of trying to "top this"—that's merely your ego talking.

- Make it OK to say nothing. Just being in a place of quiet support may make it possible for others to generate helpful ideas.

If things get off track

If the meeting tone drops or people lose the creative spirit, intervene. Any of the approaches discussed in Chapter 17 may be appropriate. But if all else fails, stop the meeting when it runs out of gas.

Summing up

Brainstorming is a specific application of the principles presented in this book. The key is that you help people stay in a healthy state of mind so they can access original, creative Thought. Creativity is not restricted to the chosen few. EVERYONE has the resources to access creativity. To keep the creativity flowing in a brainstorming meeting, watch the tone like a hawk. Insecurity and ego rapidly inhibit the process.

The most beautiful thing we can experience is the mysterious. It is the source of all true art and science.

—Albert Einstein

A suggestion

You have now covered A Foundation for Understanding and the Dynamics sections of this book. The very nature of insight and realization invites you to read those chapters more than once. Each time you read chapters, you will find you learn something more. That base of understanding about the principles that are the foundation of this approach is essential to becoming effective in directing meetings to more effective levels. There is really no end to how deeply you can understand these principles.

Coming up...

In the next section, Mechanics, we look at some of the familiar mechanics of meetings in the light of this understanding. In the next chapter, I will start with whether to even call a meeting.

MECHANICS

14

TO MEET OR
NOT TO MEET
A Classic Question Worth
Remembering

If you take a moment to reflect, you will realize the obvious: A meeting is not always the best use of time. It is worth asking whether a meeting involving several people is appropriate. Often a brief phone call or one-on-one is more expedient. Scheduling appropriate and relevant meetings helps people keep a clear head and come into your meetings with a mindset that points toward the healthy use of Thought, and results!

Before we begin discussing how to determine whether a meeting is necessary, I'd like to repeat what I said in Chapter 1 about my meaning for the word "meeting." For purposes of this book, I am defining a meeting as a scheduled gathering of more than two people. I am also excluding what we might call informal or casual meetings. Obviously, if you drop in on another manager with a question or comment, the items we are discussing in this MECHANICS section will generally not apply. Of course, everything else in this book about the human factor applies to people, period!

To meet or not to meet

In cultures, like ours, that are meeting-prone, any question, problem, incident, opportunity, and decision is cause for a meeting. One of the most often neglected questions in such cultures is whether a meeting should even be called. There are exceptions, of course, such as a VP in a large restaurant operation who told me that their senior staff meets only quarterly. The CEO will not allow any item on the agenda that requires a decision. His reasoning, I'm told, is that he expects his executives to make these decisions daily—not bring them to committee. He expects time that would otherwise be spent in meetings to be spent in the field, close to the customer.

There is no right or wrong about how many meetings to hold. However, I feel that it is useful to ask the right questions in the beginning:

- Does a meeting seem to be the best way to handle this issue?
- What do I expect to accomplish with a meeting?
- What is the possible downside if we do not have a meeting about this topic?

These and similar questions take managers out of the "automatic meeting" mode.

When is a meeting inappropriate?

Here are some examples of times when I DO NOT feel a meeting is the best choice. You may not agree, but I ask that you consider the reasoning.

When you want to convey information

To convey information, it may make the most sense to do so with an E-mail, memo, fax, intranet message, or phone call. It may be appropriate to call a meeting to clarify what was written or to communicate information that is too sensitive to put in writing. But I respectfully suggest that, as a general rule of thumb, it is not a good use of employee time to call a meeting just to communicate and digest routine information. Examples of routine information could be the latest company stock price, public notice of acquisition, an all-employee memo from the CEO, new legal guidelines, or minutes from the last meeting.

On the other hand, E-mail and memos often do not convey sentiment and context well, and they don't necessarily lead to mutual understanding. In fact, these methods can sometimes lead to misunderstanding and unnecessary confusion. That's where a meeting or at least a phone call is helpful. If you are disseminating information that could possibly be misunderstood, then consider holding a meeting. Examples of this type of information could include a pending merger, reorganization, changes in employee benefits, or any items that might possibly lead to insecure thinking and speculation.

When you feel you should involve everyone in a decision

There are many decisions that do not require a group. In the name of consensus management, however, many managers now want to throw every decision into a meeting. As we discussed in Chapter 11, there are various levels of decisions, and some are handled best in a meeting of the appropriate people. For example, you might want to have a meeting with your direct-report managers about a strategic change of direction for the company. But a well-written memo may be most appropriate for lower-level employees.

You might want to ask yourself questions like these:

- Will anything I might hear in a meeting affect my decision?

- Will this decision or information possibly cause backlash?

- Is this a decision where we need consensus; that is, a decision that everyone can live with, even if they don't agree with it?

- Is this a decision I am willing to let the group make?

- Is this the type of information that needs context and personal reassurance that would be difficult to communicate in written form?

If the answers to all the questions are no, then you might be better off NOT putting this item into a meeting. If the answer to even one question is yes, then you might consider holding a meeting, with or without issuing written information in advance of it. One example might be that the CEO has issued an edict that all department budgets be shaved 7% for the new fiscal year. Rather than announce the CEO's directive in a meeting, you might issue a memo prior to holding discussions with each department about how to implement the directive. In the memo, you might ask managers to come to the meeting with ideas about how to accomplish this goal.

When is a meeting appropriate?

Meetings are most often appropriate for situations that involve or require any one or more of the following factors:

- rapid update
- sensitive communications
- urgent, time-dependent information or emergencies
- teamwork and networking
- consensus (a meeting of the minds)
- creativity and fresh ideas
- decisions requiring input from those affected
- trial balloons

Let's look at these factors in more detail.

Rapid Update

Some situations change so rapidly that written communication is too slow. An example might be a daily production meeting in which different elements of an operation must coordinate equipment and manpower.

Sensitive communications

You may need to communicate certain information that is far too sensitive to trust to the memo or E-mail route. For example, discussions about mergers and acquisitions are sensitive, particularly in their early stages. Another application of a meeting is putting out information that requires a context to be understood in perspective. For example, the company may be planning a long-range restructure to reduce layers of management. Without the proper context and time frame, people may panic at the notion of reducing the number of jobs before they understand how it will be done. A well-run meeting allows you to handle these issues on the spot.

Emergencies

Certain urgent situations require ad hoc, emergency meetings. There is no time to make out agendas or meeting notices. Action is required immediately.

Teamwork and networking

In large organizations, managers often find themselves out of daily contact with colleagues. This is especially true in the growing trend of telecommuting. Day-to-day cooperation between managers depends on the right environment, which is why bringing these managers together periodically can do a lot in building a team spirit—if the meeting is done right. The key to these particular meetings is in-depth, respectful listening.

Consensus

In my experience, there is no better way to reach a meeting of the minds than with a well-run meeting geared for respectful listening and understanding. It is not necessary that everyone be in agreement, as long as everyone is in alignment. The difference between alignment and agreement is vast. When people agree to take a certain action, they may simply have deferred to your position. In that case, implementation may be slow or subtly sabotaged. When people are in alignment, they are of like mind. They are aligned with the vision you have presented and have risen beyond their own considerations, which may require a considerable shift in the thinking of some people. This usually takes more time; however, implementation will be relatively rapid because people are willing.

Creativity

There is no substitute for the creative synergy that a high-tone, inspiring meeting can achieve. However, a poorly run meeting can become a discouraging confirmation that creativity is dead. We discussed how to optimize creativity in Chapter 13

Decisions requiring input

Many decisions require the input and buy-in of various people. Some decisions can be delegated to a group or committee. See Chapter 11 for more on the various aspects of handling decision-making appropriately in meetings.

Trial Balloons

Sometimes a manager may be considering something so new and divergent from tradition that he or she wants to register initial reaction from a group. Participants' reactions and questions will be valuable in crafting the final release of the new ideas.

These categories do not represent the only occasions to have meetings, but they do cover the vast majority. My purpose here is to suggest that before you automatically schedule a meeting, you might *consider questioning what you expect to accomplish and whether a meeting is appropriate at all*. A wise friend once pointed out that asking the right questions is the key to fresh thinking. The answers will take care of themselves.

Summing up

Asking whether a meeting is the best format to accomplish what you want can eliminate a significant percentage of meetings. Too many managers and supervisors are already spending the majority of their workweek in meetings, less than half of which produce meaningful results. Even if a meeting seems the most appropriate medium, taking time to reflect on it will help you set up the most effective meeting.

Reflective leadership is improvisation toward a general sense of direction.
—Harlan Cleveland, US Ambassador

Coming up...

Discriminating in a good way. Sometimes the person calling the meeting invites anyone he thinks might have a remote interest in the topic. Choosing the participants needs careful attention—just as a chef carefully chooses the ingredients for her recipe. Next we examine how to decide who should attend your meeting.

15

WHO SHOULD ATTEND
Time To Get Off Automatic

> Invite the fewest people necessary to accomplish your purpose. Include only those who can contribute, benefit, or have a piece of the action.

The question of who should attend a meeting may be a familiar one, but it merits review in light of the understanding I have been discussing in this book.

Why take time to thoroughly consider who comes to meetings?

The answer to this question becomes clear when we go back to my original definition: *A successful meeting is one in which the purpose is accomplished **and** people feel good about the time they spent.*

Results and uplifting tone are the name of the meeting game. In general, the higher the meeting tone, the more is accomplished and the better people feel about the time they spent. From previous chapters (especially Chapter 8), you will recall that the tone is simply a measure of the group's mental state from moment to moment. It is an indicator of the level of creativity and common sense accessible to the group at any moment. The tone will naturally tend to rise when over-analysis, fear, and personal interests don't drag it down. A meeting of ponderous, analytical thinkers is not likely to generate an uplifting, inspirational tone. A meeting of political pundits is more likely to result in turf wars than in wit and wisdom. On the other hand, a few people who can take themselves lightly can serve as leavening agents for the mix.

Giving the attendance list some thought

People get invited to meetings for many reasons. There are those people who can contribute, those who need to be kept informed, those who might get upset if left out, and those who are always invited out of habit. Still, choosing the makeup for a meeting deserves some thought. Although some meetings, like the CEO's regular staff meeting, will usually include the same people, special meetings don't. No one can tell you who you should include, but here are some basic questions to consider as you make up the list:

- What do you want to accomplish in the meeting?

- Who can contribute to this meeting, and who can benefit from it?

- Who will work together best in this meeting to create the perfect recipe for success?

Creating the perfect recipe

The composition of the group is like a fine recipe. The ingredients that each person contributes in terms of experience, creativity, and, most important, his or her prevailing state of mind, are critical to the outcome. The type and number of ingredients you choose will depend on what you plan to accomplish in your meeting.

If your purpose is to achieve a meeting of the minds, then the smaller the group, the easier it will be. It often makes sense to achieve consensus with a small group of strong opinion-makers, and then expand it later.

If your purpose is to brainstorm new ideas, then you will want to include those folks who easily jump beyond egos into the creative mode and enjoy leapfrogging ideas with others. You may want to leave out the people who traditionally rain on the parade or need to dominate and be the focus of attention.

If your purpose is to get the latest update on people's assignments, then include only those who have a stake in the results. If it is to solve a particular problem, invite those who might contribute to the solution. If the purpose is to marshal a task force to launch a particular effort, invite those who need to know.

After you have made up your list of participants, you might want to put it aside for a day, then return to the list and go through it one more time, asking why you are including each person and making any appropriate deletions or additions.

To invite or not invite

In my experience, leaders tend to invite too many rather than too few people to meetings. When your meeting notice goes out, you will have plenty of opportunities to consider omissions when staff call and ask why so and so was not invited. It's much easier to invite later than to uninvite.

Many organizations have people who want to be included in too many meetings because they don't want to miss anything. If they will not contribute to accomplishing the goal of the meeting, leave them out but copy them on the results.

Feel free to tell these people that you are intentionally limiting the number of participants so that the meeting will stay small and flexible. After all, if you invite one or two people who detract from the meeting, you risk hurting the effectiveness of the overall group—and wasting the valuable time of everyone. In that sense, the overall good of the group takes precedence over the personal desires of the individual.

If you are in doubt about someone, do not include this person on the attendee list, but send him or her a notice of the meeting with a note along these lines: "The list of attendees includes people I feel are most directly affected by and contributing to the issues to be discussed at the meeting. For that reason I did not include you. However, if you see a reason for attending, you are certainly welcome to join us."

Adding creativity to the mix

Besides excluding certain people or combinations of people in your meeting, you can also invite certain people because of what they can add. For example, you might invite the creative head of the art department to your meeting—not because she knows much about a particular topic, but because she can bring a lighter perspective to the subject. In such cases, you can tell her in advance that you are not looking for technical input from her, but rather her contribution of humor and creativity. After a little practice, you can begin to compose the meeting makeup with the same care a fine chef does to prepare a gourmet meal. Each ingredient has a purpose. If one is required for substance but produces an off-note, another will be added to correct the flavor.

Summing up

The makeup of the meeting is a critical first step in designing a successful meeting. It is worth thinking carefully about who you invite and how they will contribute to or detract from your meeting's success, as well as how they will benefit from attending.

Planning is essential. Plans are worthless.
—Winston Churchill

Coming up...

Putting them on notice. In the next chapter, we will discuss the importance of letting people know more than just when and where you are having the meeting. Setting the meeting stage in advance is a vital step toward crafting a high-performance meeting.

16

GIVING NOTICE
Getting Off on the Right Foot

An effective meeting notice requires that the person calling the meeting think through the purpose and objectives and encourage attendees to come prepared to contribute. More fundamentally, the meeting notice should point the participants toward healthy, productive mental states.

Unless the meeting is an emergency, the participants deserve a written notice that spells out the basic who, what, why, where, when and how information about your meeting. Done properly, the meeting notice helps set the tone for the meeting. It lets the participants know what you want from them, and it gives them a chance to come prepared to contribute. Also, it forces the person calling the meeting to focus on what he or she wants to accomplish. One of the most common complaints cited by participants is no clear understanding of the purpose of the meeting, desired outcomes, and what is required of them. When participants understand, in advance, what is planned and what is expected of them, they enter the room expecting a well-run, productive meeting, and they tend to establish a higher tone at the start.

Commonsense basics

Although it may seem obvious, meeting notices often do not include the basics. How often have you received a note from your secretary such as "The Planning Meeting will be held today at 3:00 PM"? With all that information, your response would likely be "Yeah, and...?"

To avoid subjecting others to this type of cryptic announcement, here are the essential elements of effective meeting notices.

Title

The title of the meeting gives the reader the first clue about its purpose. The more specific the title, the better.

Where and when

The when and where is something often taken for granted, because the meeting is usually held in the same place. But in large organizations, meeting rooms are often scheduled for different purposes. It is just common courtesy to remind people where the meeting will be held. Telling people how long you want them allows participants to schedule their time more effectively. Even if you do not finish your business, honor that time frame and schedule another meeting if needed. Over time, you will get better at estimating how long you should need for your meeting. A real cap on the meeting time tends to motivate the meeting leader to keep things on track and participants to contribute constructively, instead of digressing into side issues or endless fault-finding.

Artists tell me that painting with a limited palette of colors forces them to become more creative. I think the same thing happens with short meetings that honor time commitments. **I recommend that meetings last no longer than one hour.** Why? It is my experience that meetings lasting much longer than an hour tend to drag and wear people down. The more people drop into low-tone mental grinding, the less productive meetings become. At the very least, it makes sense to give participants a break at the end of every hour.

Who

Listing everyone who is invited eliminates much misunderstanding. In larger organizations, especially where there is a lot of insecurity and resultant politics, some people place stock on meeting inclusion. The notice clarifies, based on its purpose and agenda, the appropriateness of who should attend.

One of my clients, the Chairman of the Board of a large conglomerate, told me that when he took over, his senior staff meetings comprised over 30 people. The 15 division presidents and senior corporate staff sat at the main conference table. Behind them hovered a row of an equal number of support personnel—just in case the senior person didn't have all the answers. The awkward size and the waste of staff hours disturbed the Chairman. It might have been more straightforward to just issue a memo requesting that only the officers attend, but this was not his style. Rather than make a direct issue of it, he asked the CFO to set up a computer terminal on the sign-in table at the next meeting. As participants entered their employee number, the screen displayed in large figures the minimum amount per hour that the company was spending on the meeting in terms of the total salaries of those present. By the next meeting, the second tier stayed in their offices—and presumably did something worthwhile.

Purpose /agenda

It is useful to have a purpose statement or an agenda. That way, people have some idea of the results expected from the meeting. The statement of purpose requires the person calling the meeting to get clear on what he or she wants from the meeting. Many clients have told me that the problem with weekly or monthly committee meetings without agendas is that they tend to accomplish just what was on the agenda—nothing. Depending on the company and the level of manager, meetings can consume anywhere from 30 to 80% of a manager's day. When managers spend a large part of the day in meetings that had no stated purpose or did not accomplish their purpose, they end up feeling like the day was misspent.

Preparation

Including a section in the meeting notice on preparation may seem unnecessary and even an insult to the attendees. Yet letting people know what you expect in advance is helpful. In my days in manufacturing, there were countless meetings in which most of us showed up having read the background material on an issue. But because a few "did not have time," we would find ourselves going over the background information during the meeting—and wasting the time of those who had prepared. Repetition of this scenario soon teaches people that it is not worthwhile to prepare in advance.

On the other hand, when you operate from the assumption that people come prepared, they soon will. One of my colleague's clients has found that setting up rules of engagement for meetings is helpful. One of the rules he champions is that only people who have read the background material are allowed to participate in the discussion or ask questions. (See "Suggested Ground Rules for Meetings" in Resources at the end of the book.)

Materials required

If you want people to have certain records or information available during the meeting, tell them in advance. It's a waste of time to wait for someone to get a document.

Notice

It is helpful to give as much advance notice as possible when you send out the meeting notice. In most organizations, one to two weeks should be adequate. Even if a meeting is required on short notice, however, a thoughtful meeting notice is worth the effort.

Let's look at two sample meeting notices.

The first example is a special meeting with one major agenda. The notice lets everyone know what he or she will discuss, what to bring, how to prepare, and what outcomes are expected. Anyone reading this notice will instantly see that the person calling this meeting has thought it through and will most likely achieve the desired outcomes.

This second example pertains to a meeting that the General Manager schedules with her staff on a regular basis. Because the notice is specific about topics for discussion, preparation, and materials required, staff can come prepared to get results. In this case, I have not listed expected outcomes because it is often difficult to predict which issues can be resolved in one meeting at this level.

SAMPLE MEETING NOTICE #1
New Customer Product Potential
called by
Ron Jones, Sales Manager

When
Tuesday, January 16, 9:30-10:30 AM

Where
Sales Conference Room 2

Who is invited:
Bill Smith (Mfg), Kim Johnson (R&D), Ken Harrier (Marketing), Jane Black (Sales), Robert Hiller (Process Eng.)

Purpose
- To determine whether we can develop products for a potential new customer.
- To establish a timetable.

Preparation
Please come prepared to discuss current R&D availability to modify existing products, Process Engineering response time for modifications, and Manufacturing capacity and delivery estimates. The attached call report provides the basic background information you will need.

Materials required
- Samples of competitive products (Black)
- Current manpower availability for this target of opportunity (Smith, Johnson, Hiller)

Desired Outcomes
- Decision on whether we can service the requirements of this new customer

  Best-case scenario

  Worst-case scenario

  Alternate interim options
- Assignment of responsibilities
- Timetable that can be calendared and assigned

SAMPLE MEETING NOTICE #2

Monthly Staff Meeting

called by
Allyson Ryan, General Manager

When
Monday, February 6, 9 AM – 11 AM (short break at 10)

Where
Main Conference Room

Who is invited:
Senior Staff, General Counsel

Agenda
1.0 OLD BUSINESS

    1.1 Progress report on plant expansion (Johnson)

    1.2 Report on law suit (Whitney)

    1.3 Report on quality plan implementation (Haggerty)

    1.4 Review of last month's action items (Allison)

2.0 NEW BUSINESS

    2.1 New market opportunity (Mathews)

    2.2 Production problems on line A (Brown & Johnson)

3.0 EDUCATION

    3.1 Results of Employee Morale Survey (Hernandez)

Preparation
Read the enclosed "New Market Opportunity" report by Mathews, dated January 15.

Materials required
- Whatever will expedite and clarify any portions of the agenda that pertain to you.
- A one-paragraph (maximum) written statement of your assessment of your department's morale. We will discuss these statements in light of Item 3.1.

Summing up

An informative, timely meeting notice is usually appropriate—and always helpful. Letting people know in advance what you want from the meeting and how they can contribute starts the group on an upbeat path toward results. Remember that every part of the meeting is designed to set the tone for the meeting. In this case, the meeting notice shows the staff that you know what you want and intend to run a meeting leading to results and an experience of time well spent.

Leaders who win the respect of others are the ones who deliver more than they promise, not the ones who promise more than they can deliver.

—Mark A. Clement

Coming up...

Are minutes really important? How much do we need to document? In the next chapter, I will get to the essence of what makes common sense when it comes to documenting a meeting—when minutes are appropriate and when are they not.

17

DOCUMENTING THE MEETING
Brief and to the Point

After a meeting, it can be useful to write up a summary of follow-up actions, main items discussed, and results. The key is to be brief and to serve a purpose. Voluminous records are seldom worth writing or reading.

A good set of appropriate, brief minutes can reinforce what the meeting accomplished and who agreed to take what actions. Few people read verbose minutes so it makes sense to keep them short and very sweet.

To document or not

When deciding to write up the minutes of a meeting, the first question to ask is whether a record is appropriate. Some meetings do not require a permanent record. Brainstorming sessions, production control meetings, and ad hoc committees may not need anything. There is no point in writing something about a meeting if it does not serve some purpose.

Some meetings of a sensitive nature are better left undocumented—especially in today's litigious society. Examples might include preliminary discussions about mergers and acquisitions, discussions about new products, and certain personnel matters. If you decide the meeting should be documented, then the next question is, for what purpose.

If your purpose is to remind people of actions they've agreed to take, then an action reminder memo works better than formal minutes. (See the example below.) Action reminders jog the memory of people who have agreed to take certain actions by specific deadlines. I recommend that you send out these reminders within two or three days of the meeting so that people have a chance to take timely action before the next meeting.

ACTION REMINDER

JANUARY 10 QUALITY COMMITTEE MEETING

Person Responsible	Action	Deadline
Ann Crawford	Obtain specs; begin employee briefing	Monday, January 16
Bill Manfred	Write procedure for statistical sampling of incoming supplies	Wednesday, January 18
Lee King	Meet with operators for feedback about quality	Wednesday, January 25
Peggy Veltroy	Prepare mock-up of possible quality newsletter	Next meeting, Tuesday, February 14

Timing your minutes

When should minutes be sent out? The answer will vary, depending on the organization and the meeting. In general, if there is to be another meeting of this same group, then send out the minutes with the notice for the next meeting. If you have already issued an action reminder, you may not need to send minutes at all; you have already summarized the key action items of the meeting two to three days after the fact, and people don't need to read about what they just attended. On the other hand, if the meeting happened a month ago, it is sometimes useful to briefly review what happened before you enter today's meeting. In that case, a brief set of minutes sent out with the notice for the next meeting could prove valuable—even if you sent out an action reminder previously. But if the minutes are for legal considerations or archives, then you may not want to send them out at all. They can be made available via computer records or company intranet.

Recording minutes

A popular method of recording a meeting is the flip chart. By having someone recording highlights and action steps on the chart in front of the room, everyone gets to see what has transpired as you go. These chart pages then serve as the notes for the meeting and make it relatively easy to write up minutes—if minutes are appropriate. Another popular format is the electronic marker board that allows you to print 8½ x 11 copies of what has been written or drawn on the board. Copies of these printouts may be all that is needed for minutes.

Who gets copies

Who should get copies of minutes? While it may seem obvious that everyone who attended should receive a copy, there are often people sitting in on meetings (such as senior executives just checking in on things) who neither need nor want a copy. If in doubt, save the paper or E-mail! They can always ask for a copy later.

Minutes, not hours

Finally, how much do you need to cover in your minutes? As you will see in the sample that follows, brief minutes with leading sentences get quickly to the point. Every meeting leader and organization will have his or her personal idea about proper meeting record format. The point here is to make the minutes visually easy to read, and to the point. Except in rare instances in which detailed legal records are needed (such as the board of directors' annual meeting), minutes serve the purpose of summarizing major events and reminding the people who attended of actions agreed on. They also give a sense of the meeting to anyone who did not attend.

MINUTES OF THE SENIOR STAFF

Agenda Item	Summary
Start	Meeting started at 10:01 A.M., Tuesday, March 8, 2003
Stockholders Meeting	After a lively discussion, it was agreed that the major theme of the stockholders meeting would be technology updates in our two major product lines. Manufacturing will prepare computer-animated mock-ups to show at the meeting.
New Quality Procedure	Tom Terrents presented an overview of the new procedures in place for raising our level of raw materials screening. These went into effect at the end of last month and have already resulted in stopping two bad shipments.
Sales Update	Sales reported that sales figures are now on the upswing in all but one product line. Current problems and various solutions were discussed for stimulating sales of the Vargan line.
City Traffic	The City Traffic Engineer made a brief presentation about the city's concern with traffic jams caused by employees arriving and departing in large groups. He suggested several possible solutions. This issue will be discussed in more depth next month.
Employee Survey	Mary Johansen presented an overview of results from the recent employee attitude survey. In general, results were positive. The major area of concern seems to be increasing health care costs. Each staff member will receive a full report within two weeks, which is when Ms. Johansen expects to complete the tabulation and analysis.
Adjournment	The meeting was adjourned at 11:02 am.

Summing up

When records of a meeting are appropriate and helpful, make them brief, easy to read, and timely. Action reminders are a good way to remind people about what they have agreed to do and when. Verbose minutes seldom get read and as a rule are appropriate only for legal purposes. What has recording the meeting to do with conducting highly effective meetings? Every manager I've ever talked with likes to know that the time he or she spent in a meeting resulted in something beneficial. Good, concise documentation highlights the results of the meeting and reinforces the thought in people's minds that these meetings, indeed, are worthwhile and hopefully even enjoyable.

Either write something worth reading or do something worth writing.

—Ben Franklin

Coming up...

Finally, we get to some of the tips and tricks that you may find useful in bringing a sagging meeting tone back up to a productive level. As I stated early on, these will make little sense and have minimal impact unless you have developed an understanding of the foundation chapters.

IN CONCLUSION

18

GUIDING THE MEETING TONE
Sensing When and How to Intervene

Use the tone of the meeting as your compass. When the tone drops, there are many things you can do to guide it toward higher levels. Above all, don't just sit there, do something!

When you notice that the meeting tone is starting to drop (you will sense it), you'll need to take action if you want to keep the meeting at an effective level. *Noticing* the tone is the first critical step. The interventions discussed below are not necessarily new to meeting leaders. However, their importance may become more apparent in light of seeing meeting tone as an indicator of the group's healthy use of Thought.

Meeting tone monitor

The meeting leader is ultimately responsible for guiding the meeting tone. As my clients come to realize the critical importance of keeping meeting tone high, they often designate one or more tone monitors to assist in their meetings. In addition to the meeting leader, the tone monitor keeps an eye on the tone and signals the meeting leader when the tone drops appreciably. This second pair of eyes is particularly valuable to a meeting leader who is just learning to monitor the meeting tone. Even an experienced meeting leader has a lot to do to keep a meeting moving along, so a tone monitor is good insurance.

Tone tools

Once you allow the tone of the meeting to be your guide, you will start to see ways to influence it. Here are just a few of the ways in which you can guide the tone toward a more positive, creative level. Even if you are not leading the meeting, you can intervene for the good of the meeting. Remember, you are simply helping people get back to their naturally healthy way of using Thought.

Starting out in the right spirit

My clients span a diverse range of organizations. Here is a story from one of my clients, an Episcopal priest, that demonstrates the power and importance of setting the right meeting tone.

We had our monthly church board meeting again last night. My associate and I were marveling at the way in which about 15 agenda items could be accomplished in such a congenial and effective way in about an hour and a half! This was done with a lot of group participation and moving forward only with consensus. The result, as usual, was a list of action steps and agreed upon delegation, which will be accomplished in the intervening month. Pretty amazing!

By keeping our eyes on the spirit of our meetings, we have built a new building, gone through a parish profile process, addressed financial needs, and developed new ministries. I've known other church vestries that have had less to do, were embarrassingly divisive, completely ineffective, and deliberated until 12:30 or 1 in the morning!

One of the differences seems to be that we start each meeting with a time of Eucharist in which we spend time in gratitude for all that is good in our lives. ("Eucharist," by the way, is Greek for "thanksgiving," which is truly the overall sense of our time together.) Other clergy have asked me how we can afford to spend this half hour. I always reply, "How can we afford not to!" We have found that we can conduct business much more effectively and graciously if we stay in gratitude and make the practice of the Presence and our relationship with one another the first priority.
—Fr. Rob Bethancourt, Fullerton, CA.

This is a wise example of recognizing the importance of starting out a meeting on the right foot. For your business meetings, you may want to start with a light, "how is everybody doing" discussion, or encourage participants to share their successes since the last meeting, or even open the meeting with some humor. The object is to make sure people are light-spirited and relaxed.

Humor

Humor is a natural tone-raising agent for meetings. It is a state of mind, not a series of jokes. Humor is about seeing and appreciating the humorous side of the simplest things. If you are tense or serious about a meeting, you will probably not see humor in anything. But if you are relaxed and feeling at ease with the meeting and operating in your naturally healthy state of mind, then certain statements or facts may strike you as comical. By spontaneously sharing your observations during the meeting, you can relieve the tension and help keep the tone at a high level.

Here are two simple examples. For nine years, I served as a trustee of our local school board. During one meeting I chaired, we were intensely listening to a presentation by another school that wanted our cooperation on a particularly controversial matter. I noticed that things had turned quite serious and that my fellow trustees and I were leaning forward, scrutinizing and judging every word of the presentation. It suddenly occurred to me to remark, "You can see from our posture here that we are really into this." All of us laughed and relaxed.

At another meeting, a parent had gotten quite adamant about her position on a matter. As she finished speaking, I could sense that the tone of the room had become tight and was headed toward defensiveness. Out of instinct I remarked with a smile, "Could you be more clear about your position?" Again, this broke the tension.

These were not stand-up comic lines but spontaneous observations that struck a humorous chord in everybody and helped us relax. Humor is the sort of thing that you just have to be open to. You can't try to make up humor or it falls flat. As you get more experienced in watching the tone, humor will occur to you when you need it.

A few words of caution are in order: The difference between effective humor that raises the tone and sarcasm that can lead you into big trouble is your state of mind. When you make a humorous remark, just make sure you are not feeling threatened, defensive, or irritated with the speaker. Otherwise, what you thought would lighten things up will come across with a bite—and may well backfire. The other key element is to remain respectful. If you are not respectful, people may feel your humor is inappropriate "given the seriousness of this issue."

Planning and rearranging agenda

Arranging the agenda of the meeting—whether published or not—gives you a chance to set the stage for optimum meeting tone. It is valuable to work from agreement as much as possible. If you know that one agenda item is likely to arouse lots of controversy, it is wise not to start with it. You might want to schedule a controversial item after an easier item that will get the meeting started off on the right foot. You will get a running start on the difficult subject. On the other hand, you probably do not want to leave that touchy item for the end when people are fatigued.

If you have an item that requires attention to a lot of detail, you might want to schedule it early in the meeting, before people get too tired. You can also split up such topics into segments and place some lighter topic in the middle for a breather. For example, you might break up next year's budget discussions with talk about the company picnic.

Sometimes you may find that even though you thought the order you established before the meeting would work, things are bogging down as the meeting progresses, Just move on to a lighter, simpler piece of business rather than tackle the next agenda item, which looks to be more difficult. Again, you are regulating the tone so that you have the best shot at starting each item of discussion in the best group frame of mind.

As for the number of items on the agenda, it is far more productive to limit the scope of a meeting so that you can keep it short. At the very least, plan breaks between major segments to give people a chance to clear their heads and come up for air.

Reframing statements: solution orientation vs. problem fixation

Some people have a habit of saying things in meetings that tend to bring down the tone—sometimes right down to depressing. Out of habit, these people can cast the most hopeful event in gloom. (It is just a habit, not a plot to destroy your meeting.) However, you can counteract their effect on the meeting tone by recasting what they've said in a more positive light.

Let's say that the CFO reports: "Profits have dropped significantly over the past three months. My projection is that the company will be in the red in 90 days. We will have to start laying off people very soon."

Obviously, such a statement will cause a noticeable drop in the meeting tone (oh yes)—bringing out insecure, reactive thinking in people. Feeling the drop, you might restate his remarks along these lines: "So if I understand you correctly, we are on a downward trend that needs attention. Since it is much easier to increase sales than cut expenses, it sounds like we need to put a special effort into increasing short-term sales. Anybody have ideas?" The concept here is to keep the tone up so that people can approach problems in a creative, proactive state of mind. People are more likely to become eager, inspired, and productive when they are given the choice to focus on solutions than when they are bogged down in problems.

Work groups

Most managers are already familiar with the concept of work groups, but I'll briefly cover it in the context of meeting tone.

Occasionally you may find that a meeting is so large that it becomes unwieldy. At other times with a large group, the opinions are so varied that it looks as though it will take far longer to accomplish things than time allows. These are times when breaking the meeting into smaller work groups might be just the ticket. You can give each small group a particular item to work on.

For example, suppose the meeting is about launching a new product. Attending the meeting are representatives from sales, marketing, advertising, finance, product development, process engineering, and manufacturing. So many steps are involved in the new product process that you might decide to break the meeting into two or three groups. In one corner of the room, you might have sales, marketing, advertising, and finance meet together to determine pricing and promotional strategies and timetables. In another corner, product development, process engineering, manufacturing, and quality assurance can put their heads together to discuss developing and manufacturing the product.

After a half hour, the groups might come back together to report their findings to the entire group. The division into smaller groups usually enlivens the tone and reduces the time required for resolution. And the shorter the meeting time, the more chance you have of keeping the tone high.

Breaks

Too often meetings just charge ahead because of limited time. Meeting leaders often keep going when they would be wise to take a break. What's the point of pressing on if the meeting tone has dropped into that grinding mode where little will be accomplished? After a particularly controversial item or one full of details that require analysis, people often get fatigued. They need a short break to change the pace. Even a five-minute coffee break or stand-up break to allow side conversation can bring a fading tone back up to a productive level.

Ending early

It is often better to end a meeting early and reschedule it if the tone won't stay at a constructive level. The point of a good meeting is to use the participants' time effectively. Sometimes, no matter what you try, a meeting will not get off the ground and become productive—or a productive meeting becomes mired in endless analytical thinking and nothing is effective in restoring a high tone. It's better to end the meeting and reschedule it than grind on and send people away feeling it was a waste of time. In any event, I think you will find that one-hour meetings work best. If you can't limit the meeting to one hour, at the very least take a break every hour.

Summing up

Intervening when the tone drops makes sense. With a little practice, you will be able to sense the differences in tone from moment to moment and guide your meetings so that participants enjoy the experience and feel it was time well spent. An array of simple interventions is at your disposal to maintain high-tone, effective meetings.

You got to be very careful if you don't know where you're going, because you might not get there.

—Yogi Berra

Coming up...

What if no one else understands this stuff? What can you do? In the next chapter, we will look at how you, as a lone voice of common sense and health, can guide any meeting to higher levels. You don't have to be in charge to make an impact.

NOTES & REMINDERS

A leader is best
When people barely know he exists
...when his work is done, his aim fulfilled
they will say:
We did it ourselves.

—**Lao Tzu**

19

YOU'RE IT!
What if No One Else Understands This Stuff?

One person <u>can</u> make a difference—for better or worse. If you are rooted in realizing the role of Thought and equipped with compassionate understanding, you will naturally be able to influence the meeting toward higher levels of functioning.

The ideal situation occurs when all meeting participants are grounded solidly in this principle-based understanding. When I have worked with an entire organization, meetings continue to get shorter and more effective because most everyone is committed to operating increasingly in their innate state of mental health. The motivation for this commitment comes from the fact that people like the experience of functioning at higher levels. They appreciate meetings that get things done and leave them feeling uplifted.

But what if you are the only one who understands this stuff? What if you cannot get other employees to read, understand, and follow the direction of this book? Can one person still make a difference?

We all know that one person in a meeting who is negative, sarcastic, or filled with ill will or self-interest can and does bring the tone of the meeting down. Everyone who attends meetings has seen this in action. The real question is whether one person operating out of his or her innate health can have a positive influence on a meeting. I doubt you will be surprised to see that my answer is "YES."

Allow me to recap many of the hints I discussed throughout this book and show you how easy it is to be a positive influence in any meeting—regardless of who is in charge.

Get centered and stay there

The centered, high-functioning state of mind that I have often referred to is natural and innate. It is the default setting for any human being. You are automatically in your continuum of innate health when your personal thinking does not override it. The most common habits of thought that will pull you out of innate health are the following:

Worry is the habit of tormenting yourself with disturbing thoughts. For example, you may have a stake in the outcome of the meeting and go into it fretting about whether your interests will be addressed properly.

Judging/criticizing is the habit of forming an opinion, estimate, notion, or conclusion—usually a critical one. You might, for example, walk into a meeting having already made up your mind about the issues. This habit will close your mind and make it impossible to listen effectively.

Busy-mindedness is the habit of keeping several things on your mind at one time. This habit is widely supported in the business world due to the misguided idea that so-called multitasking is the most efficient way to get results. It is certainly the best way to experience stress. Although worry and judging can also quickly lead you to feeling stressed, a busy mind is probably the biggest stress factor. If you walk into a meeting in a mental turbo mode, you will find it hard to listen well and especially to see to the heart of issues. A wise perspective is simply not available to a busy mind.

Memory is your archive of past experiences. If you have had an unpleasant experience in a past meeting with these people, you might find yourself falling back into those memories (thoughts) and becoming incapable of seeing anything fresh.

I am suggesting that if you entertain this kind of thinking, you will experience yourself as out of your innate health. Although it may sound simplistic, the solution is to resolve not to entertain these habits and spend as much time as possible in a centered, healthy state of mind. We human beings are highly resilient. We can feel discouraged, caught up, upset, or negative in one moment, and in the next moment, we can clear our heads and be back in our innate mental health. Emergencies are a great example. The bottom line is to commit yourself to operating out of high functioning states of mind and do the best you can. When you feel yourself moving away from health, stop and do your best to drop the thoughts—stop thinking about it. With some practice you can get quite good at this.

When you are in a healthy state of mind, you tend to draw others toward their innate health. In a healthy state of mind, you see issues more clearly, more readily avoid getting caught up in reactions, and are in a position to lighten the meeting tone with common sense and humor. People tend to listen to you more openly when you are operating from your health. These can be powerful influences on any meeting.

Don't take it personally

One of the biggest sources of losing your bearings is the habit of taking things personally. This tendency will virtually always result in an emotional reaction and behavior that will exacerbate the situation. We have all been there. You might be wondering how you are supposed to not react emotionally when the attacker is focused right on you. After all, that's pretty personal. True, but your reaction/response depends on how you see it—your thoughts.

If you want to choose not to take someone's remarks or verbal attack personally, you need to be able to see the situation *impersonally.* The understanding we have been discussing in this book makes that perspective much easier. (Impersonal is the opposite of personal, but it does not mean cold and uncaring.) To remain in an impersonal state of mind (the state of innate health, which is compassionate), you must understand what is going on for the person who is attacking you. Here is the diagram we discussed in Chapter 5.

THOUGHT - REALITY CYCLE
Thought
(Conclusion) (Belief/Assumption)

↗	↘
Conclusion	**Feeling**
↑	↓
	State of Mind
Result	**(quality of thinking)**
↖	**Behavior** ↙
	(Action/inaction)

Figure 19-1

If we recognize this cycle in operation, then it is much easier to understand where this upset verbal attacker is coming from. He is clearly upset (feeling) about something (thought). His behavior is the clear result of this thinking and feeling. Let's assume in this case that he usually reacts this way when he does not get his way. So, his habitual behavior (thought) is to get angry and lash out. It doesn't really matter at whom—except perhaps the big boss. Most of the time people accede to him because they don't like the angry confrontation.

If you see what's really going on, you won't take it personally—any more than you would take the tantrum of a two-year-old to heart. The only difference in this case is that since he is an adult, you would probably think something like, "He should know better." But if you see it impersonally (that is, you see that in the human condition everyone gets into reactive behaviors from time to time), you will be much less likely to react, and you will lead him to a very different conclusion (thought) in the cycle. After all, his outburst did not have the desired result. When that happens, he may try again and up the ante. But as long as you remain centered in your health, you will not be affected. More importantly, he begins to realize (thought) that his tantrum doesn't work with you. At the very least, you avoid making things worse by reacting to his attack.

At about this point, you might be wondering if I am suggesting you become a doormat. Absolutely not. I am certainly not suggesting that you need to overlook every disrespectful, emotionally driven behavior. At some point, it might seem appropriate to tell the upset person that this behavior is not acceptable. This is not a problem as long as you are centered in your own health.

Listen, listen, listen

Back in Chapter 2 we talked extensively about reflective listening. I would like to say a bit more about this concept as it specifically relates to influencing a meeting. Riding on the foundation of the first two points I've mentioned here, LISTENING can have the single greatest impact on any meeting. As you will recall, the listening I'm pointing to is one in which you are fully present with the person speaking and have no agenda on your mind. More specifically, you have no thoughts of judgment or evaluation, no preconceptions, no thoughts about how you see the issue, and no distracting thoughts about other things you should or could be doing. You get the idea: a clear mind without any distractions.

At any point in a meeting, you, as a participant, can step in and explain that you really want to understand the speaker. Let's say that one member of the meeting is hot under the collar and adamant about his position on an issue. His behavior is beginning to polarize the group. You start off in your neutral, healthy position and ask him for clarification. If someone jumps in and takes the conversation off course or starts arguing with him, it is easy enough to tactfully request that the person interrupting wait until you are done receiving the clarification you requested. If you listen impartially and reflectively, you will begin to bring forth the underlying logic of the speaker. More importantly, the speaker will feel listened to and understood. That fact alone will change the tone of the meeting.

Let's take a real-life example and see how this understanding applies. A mid-level manager (call him Sam) who attended a leadership retreat with me here in Coffee Creek faced what he suspected would be a difficult and challenging meeting at work. Sam works in an organization with thousands of employees. A recent reorganization left the division to which his department reports in need of some major changes. As a result of the reorganization, dozens of people from other divisions were added to several of the departments in Sam's division. The division executive assigned Sam and several other department managers with the task of coming up with a new organizational structure that made sense. The executive strongly suggested that new departments might have to be created and some department managers might have to give up some of their personnel to make it work.

In this organization, power and prestige (and perhaps salary) are tied to how many people work under you. Sam had about 150 people in his department as a result of the reorganization. He was quite certain that the meeting was going to be nothing short of a pitched battle to preserve turf. Realistically, he knew that it would make sense to give away some of his people so that new departments could be created. Still, he was apprehensive about the meeting and asked me to coach him. By this time, Sam had a fairly good grasp of the principles referred to in this book. He found himself living more in his innate health than ever before. I reviewed with Sam the basics we have been discussing here. I warned him that the tone of the meeting would probably start out low and adversarial. The key was for Sam to rise above that group mindset and trust that things would work out. Here is the account of that meeting according to Sam.

> *I walked into the meeting, and as expected, every other department manager was geared to defend things the way they were. From the outset, each manager laid out why his people should be left alone. I had only occasional twinges of insecure thoughts about what might happen if I lost significant numbers of people. I just dismissed them and got back in the moment. I mostly listened for the first half hour or so. From time to time I would ask someone to further clarify his or her position.*

Amazingly, I found it relatively easy to stay in a neutral, impartial state of mind. I began to notice that things calmed down. I don't know how much I had to do with that, but I could definitely sense the tone moving to higher levels.

About that time, I saw an opportunity to express the way I saw the situation. I told the group that I had a lot of thoughts about giving up some of my people. I admitted to being a bit fearful that it would mean a loss of my position and chances for future advancement. But I pointed out that beyond all of that, I could see where we needed to change some things. The present organizational structure had become unwieldy. So, much to the surprise of everyone (since I had the most people), I stated that I thought it would make sense to break my department into three smaller departments. At first, my statement was met with stunned silence. Then, first one and then another department manager admitted that they were in the same position and offered to give up some of their people. Once that happened, the rest was simply a matter of handling the details. We had an agreement in principle.

As I reflected on the meeting later, I was amazed at how the tone of the meeting and attitude of the participants had shifted. It was seamless and invisible, but it happened. By remaining in my own health and trusting that things would work out, the tone of the meeting moved up to a point where we found ourselves working together for the greater good of the organization.

This strategy may seem incredible, but I can assure you it does work. The reason that results like this are even possible is that *everyone* wants to operate in a healthy state of mind. It just feels better, and it produces much better results.

SUMMING UP

One person can make a real difference in any meeting. The key is to maintain your bearings and see behaviors from an impersonal stance. Staying fully present (not entertaining extraneous or fearful thoughts) allows you to bring the best out in yourself and others. All it takes is watching out for thoughts that drag you away from innate health and coming back to being present. From there you see things beyond the personal to the impersonal. You become protected from taking things personally. And most importantly, you draw others toward healthier states of mind.

Give me a place to stand, and I will move the Earth.

—Archimedes

(He was speaking about physical levers, but it applies equally to the leverage of wise UNDERSTANDING.)

Coming up...

Winding up. In the final chapter, I will pull all of this together by looking at some practical results and what went into their successes.

NOTES & REMINDERS

As long as your mind is innocent and your heart is pure, you don't have to discuss details. Just act on your thoughts because pure thought will always take you in the right direction.

—**Sydney Banks**

20

PUTTING IT ALL TOGETHER:
It's Just Common Sense

Designing and leading effective meetings that are worth people's time, is simple. Listening, a healthy use of Thought, compassionate understanding, and common sense is all you need. Trust your wise instincts and don't take it personally.

Of everything you have read in this book, the most important things to grasp are the three principles governing psychological experience: MIND, CONSCIOUSNESS, and THOUGHT. The essence of these principles is as follows:

At any given moment, Thought is the governing factor in what each of us is experiencing (feeling, seeing, hearing, smelling, tasting). As our thoughts change, so does our moment-to-moment experience. The quality of our unique personal experience from moment to moment and the quality of thinking that each of us brings to any meeting really depend on our depth of understanding of the role of Thought. The deeper our understanding, the easier it is for us to see things more philosophically, the less likely we are to take things personally, and the more open we are to receiving creative solutions from our own internal source of wisdom.

Results

Clients who have adopted this understanding and general approach to meetings report excellent results. The following story from one large organization where I was part of the consulting team makes the point.

A large multi-company corporation traditionally held two- to three-hour weekly senior staff meetings with eight to ten agenda items. After the Chairman of the Board and his corporate officers attended a three-day retreat to more deeply understand the principles I have laid out in this book, they decided to take their meetings to a new level. They appointed tone monitors and resolved that meetings would last no more than one hour—although the Chairman said he couldn't see how they were going to do it. The Chairman reported later that in the first meeting they handled only three items, but they stopped anyway. In speaking individually with his staff after the meeting, the Chairman found that most of them saw that they had attempted to talk more than listen. They also realized that when they did not know what to do with an issue they tended to belabor it rather than reschedule it for another meeting when they knew more.

In their second meeting, they started listening more reflectively, and found it easier to admit when they didn't know what to do. They handled five agenda items because the more effective listening allowed people to feel understood and diminished the need to belabor the point. After a month, the Chairman reported that they were able to handle every agenda item within the hour. What the executives found they had to do was eliminate useless discussions and endless opinions that seemed to go nowhere. They had to stay more and more present and be unwilling to entertain extraneous thoughts, judgments, and rebuttals. People began to see the value of speaking only when they could bring the discussion to a wiser level or resolution. Each member of the senior team became much more aware of his or her state of mind and the resultant quality of thinking. As a result, team members found that their innate creativity kicked in more quickly. Naturally, the company presidents began to implement the same system in their own meetings. This shift in meeting culture saves valuable time and increases overall effectiveness as people continue to realize the role of Thought at deeper levels.

Simplicity itself

If everything we have talked about in this book strikes you as simple common sense, then you are tracking with me. It is simple—it is just not so common! You will probably find it helpful to read the FOUNDATION FOR UNDER-STANDING and DYNAMICS sections several times to deepen your understanding. As you do, I know you will get better and better at guiding high-tone meetings that produce results and leave people feeling good about the time they spent.

A final thought

Now that you have made it through to the end, a few things may have occurred to you. First, you may now realize that Thought is far more pervasive and powerful than most people even dare to suspect. It is, in fact, the architect of our entire personal experience. Second, it may have struck you that this book is about far more than just meetings. The foundation of this book is about life itself and the human experience that each of us creates. To me, one of the great hopes for all of us is that we have been given the means to change our experience in life by simply using our free will to change Thought.

I have seen organizations transform simply because people at all levels in the organization realized that living and working in health is not only possible, but also profitable and fun.

My colleagues and I have seen countless success stories. Kevin Gleason's story about Adam's Outdoor Advertising in the Foreword to this book is a great example. In the midst of a five-year business recession, he turned around his company—from a book value of essentially nothing to hundreds of millions. He attributes that success primarily to the power of the understanding about the principles that I have discussed in this book. In fact, Kevin says that every dollar he invested in training returned ten dollars to the bottom line.

Imagine an organization whose core values are unconditional respect, compassionate understanding, mutual support, happiness, and service. When I have posed this scenario to groups of senior-level leaders, they often counter with "What about results?" After more than 20 years of working with all types of organizations in a wide variety of industries, I can assure you that positive results *always* flow out of a healthy organization. It's just common sense. If people spend significantly less time each day worrying about themselves and indulging in insecure thinking, they naturally focus on their jobs. In that healthy state of mind, people see to the heart of issues more quickly and have greater access to wisdom and creativity. A leader's job then becomes pointing the way and serving employees and customers.

If you would like to move the culture of your organization in the direction I've been pointing to in this book, please contact me. You can reach me most conveniently through our website (www.life-education.com) or by E-mail to rkausen@life-education.com. If you would like to deepen *your* own understanding so that you can be a more potent influence for health and wisdom in your organization, consider a leadership retreat with me here in Coffee Creek, California. You can call 530/266-3235.

Thanks for taking the time to consider this understanding.

Robert Kausen

Man's mind stretched to a new idea never goes back to its original dimensions.

—Oliver Wendell Holmes, Jr.

RESOURCES

SUGGESTED MEETING RULES

1. Without a leader and agenda, there will be no meeting.

2. The meeting leader will start and end the meeting on time.

3. The meeting leader is responsible for keeping the meeting on track and the meeting tone at the highest possible level.

4. The meeting leader will appoint a tone monitor for the meeting.

5. People who have not read the background materials before the meeting may not take part in discussions on those items. However, they may vote on any issue.

6. The meeting leader or a designated representative is responsible for issuing action reminders within three days of the meeting. Minutes, if appropriate, will be published within a week or will be attached to the next meeting notice of this group.

7. We will do our best to listen openly and respectfully in order to truly understand one another's position or communication—regardless of whether we agree.

8. We will wait after someone speaks to be certain that he or she has finished before we speak.

9. For each agenda item, a specific brief time will be allotted for discussion. Participants will do their best to deepen the discussion by listening to the heart of issues and using creative thinking and common sense.

10. For group consensus decisions, the group will move to a meeting of the minds—where participants can at least agree to disagree. If even one person cannot live with the decision, we will listen more deeply to that person until he or she feels understood.

Resources For Further Learning

Books and recorded programs

Please go to http:// www.life-education.com and click on the link to books, video and audio programs.

Customized and general business programs

Life Education®, Inc. offers private retreats for senior leadership of organizations and on-site programs for all employees. In addition, we offer numerous audio and video programs. We design all of our programs to deepen the principles and commonsense understanding that forms the foundation of this approach.

For current information on programs, please visit our website at http://www.life-education.com, or contact Life Education®, Inc at:

HCR 2 Box 3969, Trinity Center, CA 96091, phone 530/266-3235, or E-mail rkausen@life-education.com.

Public programs

Robert Kausen, Elsie Spittle, and Roger Mills, Ph.D. offer public programs through their company, Health Realization Seminars, LLC. These programs are available to the general public in various locations throughout the US and Canada. For information on programs, call 1-800-HRS-0411 (800/477-0411) or visit our website at www.health-realization.com.

LEADERSHIP RETREAT

What is it?

The Leadership Retreat is a private time for you to grow as an individual and leader. It is a unique opportunity to disengage from the daily demands and responsibilities of leadership, to take stock of your assets, and to learn something new about working and leading even more effectively. It is a perfect opportunity to prepare yourself for your next step in leadership.

What's in it for you?

You will be exposed to a powerful new understanding about the discovery of three principles that describe and define the internal, spiritual origins of the human experience. These principles represent the dynamic process, moment-to-moment, by which people generate and know their life experience. As your understanding deepens, you will realize:

- what really makes people tick: the definitive role of thought in experience
- the key to richer relationships
- how to have an even more effective 'bedside manner' while still being firm and decisive
- how to reduce stress dramatically while increasing effectiveness
- how to access wiser vision and perspective
- how to bring out the best in anyone (even marginal performers), and foster creativity
- how to access high levels of "flow" or "zone" performance
- how to foster effective teamwork and consensus without endless meetings
- how to establish and lead a healthy, high performance organizational culture
- how to more effectively separate your job from your family life

How does it work?

You will be coming to Coffee Creek, located in the majestic Trinity Alps wilderness area of Northern California where you will work privately with Robert Kausen, a highly experienced coach for leaders.

In learning sessions each day, you will begin to realize a deeper understanding of the three principles, Mind, Consciousness and Thought. As you begin to quiet down and become more centered, you will recognize misunderstandings, blind spots, mental habits and assumptions that may be limiting your effectiveness. You will rediscover how to access innate healthy thinking that produces creativity, perspective, and effective interpersonal skills. Between sessions you will be watching instructional videos, listening to audio programs, or reading. There will be time for reflection and assimilation—so essential to life-changing insights. These defining moments mark the way to a fresh start, and remarkably greater impact as a leader.

How do you arrange for a personal retreat?

The Leadership Retreat is not a group function but a personal learning experience scheduled to meet your needs.

To discuss your situation in more depth, and to arrange a time to fit your schedule, write or call

Robert C. Kausen, President, Life Education®, Inc.
Star Route 2-3969, Trinity Center, CA 96091
Phone (530)266-3235, Fax (530)266-3933
Email rkausen@life-education.com

ADDENDUM

Answers to Commonly Asked Questions

What is the Life Education approach, and how is it different from other leadership programs?

Traditional leadership programs focus on limitations and barriers. They teach compensating and coping skills, and offer techniques and "shoulds". They attempt to fix what is wrong. They deal with the products of misused thought. Thanks to groundbreaking work in the past 20 years, we have come to realize a different understanding. People are inherently healthy and high functioning—they know how to sustain successful relationships. Chronic stress is neither normal nor necessary. Executives already have the resources for vision, diplomacy, and the art of bringing out the best in people. Anything to the contrary is the result of innocent misunderstanding and misuse of the powers of thought. The Life Education process simply corrects the misunderstanding through commonsense education about the principles that govern the human experience.

What could I learn in few days that might be helpful as a leader?

The essence of our work with leaders is to open the doors to ever-deeper levels of understanding about human psychological functioning and access to our innate health and creativity. Thought is the architect of our individual personal experience. Whatever we think is instantly made real for us via our senses. Our depth of understanding about how this works determines how well we manage the process. It determines how mentally healthy and creative we are, and how well we do in working with people.

Ignorance about this process results in believing our thinking is real, no matter how painful, distorted, or unproductive. Understanding how thought works keeps us from becoming frightened or conned by our thinking when it becomes misleading and counter-productive. Here are a few practical implications.

Stress

State of the art training offers stress management techniques based on the assumption that stress is endemic to certain jobs, situations, and people. Yet, we all know exceptions—people who are not affected. The difference lies in how they think. Understanding the connection between thought and experience frees us to handle "stressful situations" in a healthy manner that eliminates chronic stress.

Effectiveness

All people experience variations in the quality of their think-ing—we call this moods. Lower quality thinking is unproductive, sometimes leaving us feeling discouraged. Higher quality thinking brings creativity, clarity, and perspective. All thinking *appears* valid to us. Understanding these fluctuations in quality provides us the perspective not to make rash decisions from extreme highs or lows. Through understanding, we become more graceful in the continual adjustment to shifting quality of thought in others and ourselves.

Creativity

Original thought is our innate resource for creativity. Understanding how to access this more often allows us to bring fresh solutions to life's challenges. It is this capacity that allows us to see situations with broad perspective, and to become more visionary as leaders. With diminished access, we tend to grind on problems, become managers of details, and suffer from "hardening of the attitudes."

Bedside Manner

Learning to access a high impact, healthy state of mind leads to compassion and understanding in dealing with people. This natural warmth and diplomacy allows us to bring out the best in people—even when firmness is required. When we deal from an intellectual mindset, our manner with people often seems cold and aloof. This tends to put people into reaction and defensiveness—impeding performance and ability to learn and grow.

Do you recommend including my mate?

Many clients include their mate in the retreat for two reasons. First, your personal relationship will become even stronger and your mate will understand what you are learning. Second, your mate will be able to serve as a partner to help you keep on track when you get back on the job. However, including a mate is not essential to the success of this program.

What results do clients report?

My mind was so busy that I usually functioned on the brink of overwhelm. Reflection was just not something I allowed myself. I still accomplish a lot, but I am able to find more quiet times. Perhaps most important, I learned to listen. My employees now tell me they feel that I really understand them. — **COO, Health Provider**

I drove myself relentlessly for perfection and was badly stressed. My analytical approach to everything kept me from having successful relationships because there was no real human connection. I discovered a resource of innate health that I never knew existed. My work is just as good, but I am no longer stressed. **—Dentist**

I had no idea that I was so judgmental, nor did I realize that my judgments were interfering with my relationships. I have now found much more compassion for people. I see differences with a wiser perspective. I feel much closer to people and am even more effective in managing them.
—Senior Manager, Retail

I was about to be transferred or fired because my boss felt that I just couldn't get along with my peers. I was convinced that I did not have the problem, and that he just did not know how incompetent most of them were. I came to the retreat dragging both feet, but I'm glad I made it! I was stunned to see how arrogant I was. Now I listen and hear what people are saying. It even helped my marriage. **—Senior VP, Insurance**

I built my company from the original concept to a successful venture. I didn't realize that over the years I had become serious about it and my employees felt burdened. With your help, I was able to regain the spontaneity and joy I had in the beginning ... and learn to articulate my vision of this organization more effectively to my people. We're getting more done and having fun too. **—CEO, Manufacturing**

Thank you for sending back the man I married over 20 years ago!
—Wife of Senior Technology Manager

INDEX

A

accountability · 86

B

back burner· 67
brainstorming · 72,116
building blocks of the human experience · · · · · · · · · · · 43
buoyant health · 66
business programs· 179
busy-mindedness · 51,163

C

cannot live with the decision· · · · · · · · · · · · · · · · · 99,178
centered· 51,71,163,181
clearing the mind · 103
common sense · 133,164,172
commonsense understanding· · · · · · · · · · · · · · · · · 15,179
compass of feelings · 49
conflict · 62,94,100
consciousness· · · · · · · · · · · · · · · · · · · 35,44,74,172,181
consensus · · · · · · · · · · · · · · · · · · 94,97,106,126,129,178
creative flow · 120
creativity is natural· 117

D

decision · 48,51,67,73,99
decision Type · 105
decision-making · 103
distracted· 27,111
don't take it personally · · · · · · · · · · · · · · · · · · · 101,166

E

equanimity · 88

F

faith in the unknown · 68
feeling compass · 52,75,92
feeling state · 50,52
forgiveness · 85,87
free will · 48,175
further Learning · 179

H

human factor · · · · · · · · · · · · · · · · · · · 7,15,17,41,77,125
hard feelings · 99,104
hidden agenda · 106
high performance · 70,180
high states of mind · 36
high-state meetings · 37
how to get the most out of this book · · · · · · · · · · · · · 20
how we create our experience · · · · · · · · · · · · · · · · · · 43

I

ill will · 85-91,105,114,163
impartial, nonjudgmental inquiry · · · · · · · · · · · · · · · · 96
impersonally · 166
Innate creativity · 117-118
innate health · · · · · · · · · · · · · · 44,51,65-67,163-170,181
innate mental health · · · · · · · · · · · · · · · · · · · 10,66,164
insecure thinking · · · · · · · · · · · · · · · · · 18,42,74,126,175
insight · · · · · · · · · · · · · 19,26,66,72,109,110,117,120
insightful listening · 26,32
instinctive navigation · 84
intuitive navigation · 84
invite or not invite · 134

J

judging/criticizing · 163
judgment · 23,33,51,91,119,167

K

Robert Kausen · 9

L

Life Education · 10,129
limiting self-concept · 56
listening · 23
    evolving conflict · 95–96
    heart of matters · 25
    listening for insight · 26,32
    listening to clarify · 25
    listening to evaluate · 24
    listening without hearing · · · · · · · · · · · · · · · · · 24
    opinions · 109–111
losing your bearings · · · · · · · · · · · · · · · · · · · 74,101,165

M

defining a meeting · 17
meet or not · 124–125
meeting levels · 38
meeting makeup · 135
meeting notices · 138
    materials required · 141
    preparation · 140
    purpose /agenda · 140
    title · 138
    where and when · 138
    who · 139
meeting rules · 178
meeting tone monitor · 154
meeting tone · · · · · · · · · · · · · 52,78-79,121,132,153-164
memory · 8,119,164

Mind · 45,74
mindsets · 71
minutes · 145
   action reminder · 146-147
   minutes, not hours · 149
   recording minutes · 148
   to document or not · 145
   who gets copies · 148
moods · 42,71,182

N

no hard feelings · 99

O

one person can make a difference · · · · · · · · · · · · · · · 162
opinions, catapult into insight · · · · · · · · · · · · · · · · 110
opinions create a quagmire · · · · · · · · · · · · · · · · · · 110
opinions to the test · 112
original Thought · 66,116

P

principle-based understanding · · · · · · · · · · · · · · 8,17,162
peace of mind · 87
personal, making it · · · · · · · · · · · · · 46,101,112,165-166
personal experience · 44-47
personal reality · 44-47, 58
philosophical perspective · 43
power of Thought · 15,19,37
presence · 26-28
principles · 19,20,44-49
   Consciousness · 44
   everything starts with Thought · · · · · · · · · · · · · · 46
   how we create our experience · · · · · · · · · · · · · · 43
   level of understanding · · · · · · · · · · · · · · · · · · · 49

Mind · 45
Thought · 44
promote innate, creative thinking· · · · · · · · · · · · · · · 119
psychological innocence· · · · · · · · · · · · · · · · · · · 89,91
public programs · 179

R

rapport · 28, 71
reading this book, best way · · · · · · · · · · · · · · · · · · 33
reality · 59
reasonable minds could disagree · · · · · · · · · · · · · · 98,107
reflect · 119,124,130
reflective listening · · · · · · · · · · · · 24-30,71,84,95,111,167
relationships· 23,43,59,71,83
respect· 27,83-85,97
role of Thought · · · · · · · · · · · · · · · · · · 63,71,94,173,180

S

sensitive communications· 128
separate reality· 28,63
simplicity · 174
state of mind · · · · · · · · · · · 37-39,42,49,73,89,119,134,166
High states of mind are innate · · · · · · · · · · · · · · 36
staying on track · 74
stress · 44, 74, 164,182

T

thinking evolves · 19
Thought · · · · · · 40,43,53,55,66,71-75,83,89,116,166,172
changing thought · 19
limiting self-concept · 56
recognizing personal reality is thought · · · · · · · · · 58
reinforcing success · 58
Thought in disguise · 59
Thought recognition · 60

THOUGHT - REALITY CYCLE· · · · · · · · · · · 56, 89,166
three principles· 44-46,172
tone · · · · · · · · · · · 52,78-81,94,103,109-114,119,120,133
   tone of the meeting as compass · · · · · · · · · · · 153-154
tone monitor· 88,120,154,178
tone tools · 154
   breaks · 159
   ending early · 159
   humor· 155
   planning and rearranging agenda · · · · · · · · · · · 156
   reframing statements · · · · · · · · · · · · · · · · · · · 157
   starting out in the right spirit · · · · · · · · · · · · · 154
   work groups · 158

U

unconditional respect · 27,84
unknown · 68,113,119

W

worldview · 28,59-60,94
worry· 44,51, 66, 73,103,163

Z

zone · 39

VOLUME PRICES ON
We've Got To Start Meeting Like This!
$16.95

Quantity	Discount	Unit Price
2-4	20%	$13.56
5-9	30%	$11.87
10-24	40%	$10.17
25-49	42%	$9.83
50-74	44%	$9.49
100-199	48%	$8.81
200-499	50%	$8.48
500 and up	40%, -25%	$7.63

SHIPPING

Shipping is in addition. For quantities of up to 9 copies, shipping is $4.00 + 0.50/copy. For quantities of 10 or more, please contact us for shipping costs.

California residents please add 7.25% tax.

[Order form on reverse side]

LEi RAPID ORDER FORM

Fax orders: 530-266-3933
Phone orders: 530-266-3235
Postal orders: Life Education, Inc.,
HCR 2 Box 3969,
Trinity Center, CA 96091-9500
Email orders: orders@life-education.com.
Tell us what you want and we will contact
you by phone for payment options.

For single copies of this book, we suggest you try your favorite neighborhood or Internet book store.

For pricing on multiple copies of this book, please see the reverse side of this page.

Please send _____copies of
We've Got To Start Meeting Like This!

Name_____
Organization_____
Address_____
City:_____State_____Zip_____
Country_____Phone: (   ) _____
Email:_____

Enclosed is $_____[] Check [] Money order
[]Visa [] MasterCard [] Discover [] American Express
_ _ _ _ _ _ _ _ _ _ _ _ _ _ _ _ _ _ _ Exp. Date_ _ _/_ _ _

Name exactly as it appears on the card:
_____

Signature_____

[Over for volume pricing]